Praise

Communism brought decades of deep darkness to the once shining nation of Latvia. However, even in darkness God is always providentially at work. This is a story that needs to be told. Only an amazing God can take a brain tumor and use it as a seed to give birth to a vision for a life- and light-giving ministry like Talsi Christian School.

I've seen TKS first hand. I've lead summer camps there. God has worked in and through Inguna in truly startling ways. Great thanks to Ryan for bringing us the story of *God Still Moves*. I pray that you too will be encouraged that no matter what circumstances you might face in life, God still moves!

—Bruce A. Hess
Senior Teaching Pastor Wildwood
Community Church
Norman, Oklahoma

GOD STILL MOVES

RYAN T. DALGLIESH

GOD STILL MOVES

SEEING THE TIMELESS WORK OF GOD IN HER STORY, HIS STORY, AND OURS

TATE PUBLISHING
AND ENTERPRISES, LLC

Published by Tate Publishing & Enterprises, LLC
127 E. Trade Center Terrace | Mustang, Oklahoma 73064 USA
1.888.361.9473 | www.tatepublishing.com

Tate Publishing is committed to excellence in the publishing industry. The company reflects the philosophy established by the founders, based on Psalm 68:11,
"The Lord gave the word and great was the company of those who published it."

Book design copyright © 2015 by Tate Publishing, LLC. All rights reserved.
Cover design by Roland Caballero
Interior design by Jake Muelle

Published in the United States of America

ISBN: 978-1-62902-267-3
Religion / Christian Life / Spiritual Growth
15.06.02

This book is dedicated to all those men and women everywhere around the world who continue to boldly follow the one true God who saved them, sustained them, and sent them. Thanks for your legacy of faithfulness that echoes from generation to generation.

To my boys, Asher and Ryker. May you grow to love the Lord deeply.

Acknowledgments

Thanks to Inguna Gruznina. Your testimony is so encouraging and reminds us all of the beautiful work God is doing in our lives. Thanks for entrusting the telling of this story to me. Those who read this book will never be the same.

Ken, thanks for calling me on that cold December day. Thanks for your patience as we labored hard on this project. Thanks for all you do for people like Inguna and myself to keep us pressing forward with the work God has trusted to us.

Brent, your generosity to Inguna and Talsi Christian School since the very beginning is without bounds.

Bruce, thanks for taking the time to read the book and give me terrific feedback.

Emily, thanks for making me look like a better writer than I actually am.

Lezlie, Laura, Mendi, and my own sweet aunt Ann, thanks so much for being my readers and for your constant encouragement.

Lakan, thanks for your constant mentorship and wisdom.

Michele, my sweet bride, projects like this seem far less daunting with your constant love and support.

Contents

Foreword

There is a subtle feeling of condemnation that creeps in on us as we read our Bibles. We feel it when we go to church and hear the testimony of the visiting missionary. We have coffee with our friends, and they regale us with tales of how God is "working" in their lives and "speaking" to them. Everyone seems to have the huge moments with God where he explodes like a supernova—everyone except us. Where is the God from Acts? Where is the supernatural hand guiding us to do great things? Frustrated, we go home and sit on the couch with eyes tightly shut, trying to block out all the noise, all the distractions. We wonder if today might be the day God breaks through the veil and shows himself to us. We hope this will be the moment our lives rise out of mediocrity and into the stratosphere of those selected few believers who seem to have God on speed dial.

If it isn't condemnation we feel, then perhaps it is distance. We read the Bible and think about how great it is that God *used* to work so clearly, and we wish he didn't seem so far away. We are embarrassed to admit it, but we find ourselves thinking God may have been cooler in the first century than he is now in the twenty-first. We have conversations with our friends and say something like, "It is neat how God did things back then." We are aware of a gap. A chasm has been fixed—or so we think—and we feel as though the God Paul knew is somehow different than ours.

It is my hope that the book you now hold in your hands will encourage you. I don't want this book to be just another example of what God is doing in someone else's life but rather what God has done and is doing all around us—and in us. You will have to read through to the end to see that this is more than just the telling of a story from a faraway place or distant time. I will tell you the wonderful story of Inguna, a Latvian woman through whom God is doing great work. I will remind you of Paul, the prince of preachers in the New Testament and how God worked through him to leave a legacy of gospel truth. Having told both of those great stories, I'll remind you of our story, the story you and I share as the normal everyday sort of people who simply want to love God well in our daily moments of running here and there. God works the same in Inguna as he has in Paul and as he does in you and I. God's gracious work continues through the pages of history in her story, his story, and ours. I know you will be blessed as you see glimpses of deep biblical truth in the stories included in these pages.

Our God is unchanging and infinitely beautiful. The work he did then, he continues now.

Introduction

It was December 9 and unseasonably cold for Texas. The unusual amount of ice had stopped all flights in and out of our town's tiny airport for the last three days, but here I was, up at 4:30 a.m. on my way to catch a flight to Dallas. I don't like the cold at all, and I like early mornings even less. The wind tore at my cheeks and fingers as I moved gingerly over sheets of ice from the parking lot into the offensive fluorescent lights of the terminal. My eyes were more content to squint and blink, and my body protested the lack of sleep by allowing the cold to invade every joint and muscle without resistance.

What was I doing here? Why was I flying to Dallas to meet a woman from Latvia?

Five days earlier, I had received an email from Ken, a man I had met once at a youth camp. It had been nearly three and a half years since then. He wanted to call me. I was in the middle of a deliberate sabbatical and was working on a writing project. I knew if I took a call, the momentum I had gained would be lost, but I sent him my number. Two minutes later, my phone rang. Polite greetings were exchanged, and then he dove in to the purpose of his call.

"Ryan, I think people in church these days feel a disconnect from Acts. I don't think people believe God is still working like he used to. I want to change that. There is a Christian school in Latvia I've been a part of for nearly fifteen years, and I know God is still moving. I want people to remember that God is still active and alive. I think this story would help people to see that, and I want you to write it. I knew when we met that we'd work together at some point. I think this is the time. I can fly you to Dallas to meet Inguna. She is only here for another few days."

Of course, there was more to the conversation than that, but I told him I'd discuss it with my wife and let him know. I called Michele, and she said what she always says: "I don't know how you turn that down." (Because of my sweet bride and her desire that I serve God well, I have had a multitude of opportunities.)

My head was heavy and nodding on my chest. I was doing all I could to keep from drooling all over myself, and my brain was foggy with fatigue just minutes from landing in Dallas.

Wayne, a friend of Ken's, picked me up at the airport. The roads were frozen solid and buried a couple of inches deep in ice. Bulldozers scraped overpasses, and everyone being forced into one or two lanes made the normally busy traffic worse. An hour later, we picked up Inguna.

She was younger than I had expected, only in her mid-forties, and her hair was black and hung well past her shoulders with bangs curled tightly over her forehead. Her eyes were—and still are—a mystery. They were bright and full of life, maybe blue, maybe green, but her left eye had a large patch of brown in it. She was dressed smartly and struck me as completely in charge of absolutely everything.

She climbed into the back seat without smiling.

"Where is Ken?" she asked with a thick accent and a quick tone. Wayne explained Ken wouldn't be able to join us as he was preparing for a business trip. Inguna rolled her eyes. "Of course, of course, of course."

We made introductions and shook hands, and she pursed her lips while giving a polite nod and customary, "It is nice to meet you." We had nearly an hour's drive to our first meeting. I was glad to have some time with her in an informal setting and turned in my seat to face her. I was here, after all, to see if I could write a book about what God was doing in and through her ministry.

"Tell me about yourself, Inguna."

She smiled a broad smile and laughed a beautiful laugh. She was passionate, exuberant and even tearful as she began to piece together for me her history. The rest of the drive won me over. God was bringing together a West Texas preacher, a businessman, an attorney, and a wonderful Latvian woman to remind the world that our God lives and moves even today. Whatever happened next, I had to use her story to help people love God more deeply and enjoy him more fully. This book is the result.

God Works Salvation in Talsi: Inguna's Story

It was April. Precisely four months earlier, I had flown to Dallas to meet Inguna, and now, unbelievably, I was sitting in her office halfway around the world. I grabbed my green moleskin and my favorite pen. My brain was already heavy from the jetlag, but I only had three days. Three days to get the entirety of a twenty-year story. So we began.

"If you don't know anything about God, if you have not heard of the Bible, you can live your life quite well. Just live your life and be happy," Inguna said. "But I believe once in every person's life, God puts you in a situation to cry out to God. And that is what happened in my life."

She grew up in a small town called Talsi. It is a beautiful little place with brick streets winding through the oldest parts of the city. A small Lutheran church dating to the sixteenth century sits atop a hill overlooking a tiny lake, its white steeple piercing the blue sky. The countryside is blanketed in rolling farmland, green hills, and rich black soil turned up by the plow. The pine and birch grow tall and thick in any area the people haven't marked as their own and cover nearly 50 percent of the small country. Soviet-era apartment buildings like giant boxes break up the landscape of the classic European design that speaks of a time before the occupation. Ancient cemeteries mark the hillside. Each stony cross emerges from the mossy soil as a testament to those who fell in war and life, their memories fading into the fog of centuries. There are no paths there anymore. No more visitors. The city itself is restful. Peaceful. But it wasn't terribly long ago when the nation felt and wore the fatigue of the heavy Iron Curtain.

Inguna was atheistic—as was much of the rest of her country in 1990. Communism and the Soviet Union were reigning in Latvia. God and a large portion of his church had been cast into Siberia. But as far as she knew, she was happy in her life. She had a husband, Maris, who loved her. Her daughters Zane and Elina were three and one respectively. There was no thought of God in her heart. One summer morning, Elina woke up partially paralyzed. Their tiny little girl seemed so fragile and helpless. Fear swept through the young couple, and they hastened to Riga, the capital city, about 115 kilometers away. The news was deeply grim, made more so by the conditions of Soviet hospitals and doctors. It was a brain tumor. Surgery would be very complicated and would likely result in death.

"It was the first time I ever thought of life and death," she said. "I was twenty-five."

The hopelessness of the situation seared her heart like a hot iron, and tears flooded her cheeks.

"I realized that though I wanted to die instead of my daughter, I could not, and I could do nothing about this."

But then, like a small beacon of light breaking through the whelming darkness, a thought struck Inguna. A faint and faraway memory of a book came to mind. She recalled a book that spoke of the baptism of infants so the child could go to heaven. She wondered if there could be such a place as heaven. It was a small and ridiculous hope to someone who didn't believe in a god, but it was at least something.

* * *

Inguna looks up from her desk at this point and throws her head back in a smile and half laugh. We have been sitting in her office at Talsi Christian School in Latvia for a few hours now as she recalls the story of her life. She isn't anything like the young fearful mother about whom she is telling me. Now she is confident, beaming with the love of Jesus. Joy floods her face. She interjects, "Of course, now I know it isn't baptism that saves you. It's faith in Jesus. But at that point, I was willing to try anything for my little girl."

She offers me some tea and disappears for a moment. Her office is highlighted in purple. Even the binders on her shelf are purple; it is her favorite color, after all. Paintings from former students mark the walls. She hurries back into the office, directing a few final comments in Latvian to her staff before she shuts the door. Her purple jacket makes me smile. She hands me my tea, and I notice as she takes a sip of hers that her favorite purple mug says "friends." At that moment, I feel as though we really are.

Before she even retakes her seat, she says, "Okay, so where were we?" With that, we are taken back to 1990, and the joy of this moment gets washed away by the storm of the story.

*　　*　　*

"We went back to Talsi to get Elina baptized. We found an old man, at least seventy years old, and asked if he would baptize our daughter."

The man was gentle and kind. His hair was white with age. The church had been shut down, and he had been sent to Siberia in his younger days. In this moment, he was about to speak the first truth of God Maris and Inguna would ever hear. He took a large, heavy skeleton key the size of one's palm and unlocked the weighty wooden doors that towered above the young couple by a good four feet. Just past the first set of doors stood an iron gate. This was the last barrier for a heartbroken mother. She stepped into the church, cradling the small child in her arms. A short arched hallway made of stone opened into a narrow sanctuary with high ceilings. The church was hollow and empty as many churches were under the Soviet regime. Sunlight played through the windows and splashed along the floors, leaving long trails of light. A heavy gold chandelier hung in suspended disbelief that there were people here. The pulpit stood empty as it had for decades. On the back wall to the left was a man hanging on a cross, though the man and even the cross were foreign to this mother and father. How strange it all seemed. Suddenly, a tinge of fear swept over Inguna. In movies she had seen parents baptize their children, but they were always in beautiful white dresses. She was nervous to ask, "Will you still baptize Elina even though we don't have the white dress?"

"Dear child," came the voice of the old pastor, "God doesn't look at your dress. He looks into your heart." Those words were profoundly true and settled mounting tension. The pastor spoke again, "I will baptize this child, but this child of God will need godly parents. You should start going to church."

Maris's eyes met Inguna's gaze, and with eager assent, they nodded, "Yes, we will go to church. We will go!" The lie left their lips with great ease. They would have said anything to please the old pastor so long as he would baptize their daughter.

The ceremony was a simple one while three adults huddled around a small child in an empty church. A short prayer and a sprinkle of water ended it all. What a sight it must have been. But God was moving in this moment. Inguna looked up from the baptism to see a large painting on the back wall easily ten feet tall. The painting was very old, flat on the bottom and rounded on the top set inside a bright gold frame. It was a painting of the ascension, which meant nothing to her at that point. Jesus, robed in white, hovered in the clouds with his palms downturned to the eleven remaining apostles. Ten looked longingly to him with hands clasped together or reaching out; one had his eyes cast on the ground.

Inguna looked from the child in her arms to the picture of this man who must have been God: "God, if you are real, if you exist, save Elina's life, and I will serve you." It was the first time she had ever prayed. It was just a simple prayer from an unbelieving heart. Little did she know then how God would bring that prayer into play in the coming years. The whole experience was more from hopelessness than faith, and they returned to the hospital in Riga.

The next six months were difficult. During the surgery, a piece of Elina's skull was removed and never replaced so the pressure from her brain swelling would be relieved. The raven-haired mother wept as she saw the patch of skin over the wound pulse and move with her child's heartbeat.

It was forbidden that parents should stay in the hospital with their children, but Inguna wasn't going anywhere. She could only remain if she cared for the other eight children in the room. She became nurse and maid, and when she grew weary, she'd lie on the floor beneath her daughter's bed to sleep for a few minutes.

Next came the radiation treatment. It was crude and dangerous. The small toddler refused to remain still despite the urgent need to do so. Both grandmothers stepped in. They took turns holding down Elina, receiving harmful doses of radiation themselves. "They did it to protect me, so that maybe one day I could have more children." Six months came and went, and Elina went home. Christmas was sad; Elina had turned into a vegetable. She no longer moved or smiled. Everyone knew that even if she were to recover, she would have mental and perhaps physical handicaps. Each day that passed carried Elina closer to her death and Inguna further into depression.

Inguna's eyes glisten with tears as she speaks to me. The pain she felt in those days, the love from her mother and mother-in-law as they served her, weighs heavily on her even now. I'm not a crier personally, but my eyes blur with sorrow as I listen.

"My husband was busy with work, and my depression deepened. I know now that this was terrible for Zane."

A year passed. There were changes taking place as the Soviet Union began to break up. Inguna was buried under fear and sorrow, but God had never forgotten this woman or her family. In August, Inguna took a part-time job at a school; she would be working for a few hours a day. A week before school started, the teachers were there preparing for classes. The director asked the teachers if anything interesting had happened over the summer. One physics teacher named Verners spoke up. He was a bit older, probably sixty. He spoke plainly and boldly.

"I was saved this summer," he said. "I became a Christian. I am sorry that I had been an atheist."

Inguna admits she and her friends "mocked and snorted at this old stupid communist who believed in God." They knew that if he really went to church at all, it was just to receive humanitarian aid like all the other hypocrites. Last year he had been an outspoken communist. Given time, they knew he would give up this new pursuit. What a fool he seemed to them. Inguna made it her personal mission to prove to Verners that the Bible was not true.

She found a small blue Gideon Bible and began reading. Some things struck her as familiar and others as funny, but she was not impressed by this book and one day cornered the old physics teacher.

"Verners, I want to talk to you," she said as they stood next to the window at the end of the hallway. "Blood is dropping out of this book! If God is real, how could these things happen to people and little babies?" Of course her own little Elina played across her mind. She had been without any quality of life for more than a year now. Verners looked at this young mother whose eyes blazed with fire and fury.

"Inguna, I know why you are so upset, but God did not kill those babies," he said. "Human choice and sinful nature caused those things. God could stop it, but he didn't, and he knows why." He spoke with such resolve and such peace that Inguna calmed down. Still, she walked away from the conversation knowing she was completely right about the Bible. Little did she know what the coming months would hold.

It was September, and the air was already a little cooler. With the fall weather came four American missionaries. The Iron Curtain had been shattered, and the first people through were bringing with them the good news of Jesus. It didn't take long for Inguna to hear that there were Americans in Talsi. She wasn't sure what to think. In school they had been taught to hate Americans as their greatest enemies. Combat training had equipped them to kill these spiteful foes. Still, images of Marilyn Monroe from the movies flooded her brain, and she wondered if all the women looked like her.

"I just wanted to see these Americans and how they would look."

In no time, the missionaries found their way into the little building where Inguna worked. They had come to bring God, but no one cared about God at all. They just wanted to see the Americans. The teachers all gathered around to sit and to listen. It couldn't have been more perfect; God was revealing himself to those who didn't even know they wanted him. Inguna was particularly drawn to a Texan named Joann. They quickly became friendly, and Inguna asked if Joann might want to come over for dinner. Joann was delighted to eat with her new friend. Dinner was simple, and the conversation was awkward as Inguna tried to speak English.

"Would you please go with me to the Talsi Baptist Church?" Joann asked.

Inguna's mind raced. She wasn't sure what to do. Maris was working away from home. Her daughters were still so small. And to top it off, she had lived here for twenty-six years and had never even noticed a Baptist church. Thinking she ought to be kind to Joann, she agreed to the invitation and dressed the girls in their finest clothes.

The timid mother took her children to church for the first time. Anxiety swept over her. The service was nice but very foreign. The thing that struck Inguna most was when an elder Latvian woman came up to her and said, "I'm glad you came. Will you please come another time?"

Inguna was shocked. In Soviet times, one didn't talk to strangers or even act amiably toward them. She nodded her head in assent. When she went home, the weight of change was obvious. Latvia was independent, Americans had come proclaiming God, she had been to church, and a woman had actually been kind to her and invited her back. She had been seen. She had been noticed. Her word was her bond, and so she did return as she had promised the old woman. But she was still reluctant. Her promise to the white-haired Lutheran pastor still hung in her head. She had told him they would go to church.

"Maris, should we go to church?" she asked her husband, though she hoped he shared her reluctance. She was jubilant when he dismissed the opportunity due to a basketball game on television.

For the next year, Inguna was loath to attend church. She would do what everyone else did: sing the songs, bend her head to pray. She followed all the rules to the letter, but Jesus wasn't there for her yet. In a year, the willing but inept pastor had never taught that Jesus was the son of God or even spoken of the need to be saved. Inguna pressed on and continued going because she admitted she "knew it was a good thing to be in church on Sunday morning."

It was the summer of 1992, and two years had passed since Inguna stood in that Lutheran church with her frail little girl—two years since she had first heard the truth of God, two years since she had first prayed. For the last year, she had been going to church off and on and had made new friends. Inguna had been invited to go to a summer discipleship training school on the weekends. She was excited to go, but when she told Maris she would be going, he did not receive it well.

"If you had been there, you'd have seen the scandal. My husband loved me, but when I started going to church, something happened. I began to see our lifestyle didn't please God at all. We lived a very secular lifestyle—that includes everything. I tried to tell him we should change, but he became jealous. We fought constantly, and he threw a fist."

*   *   *

Inguna means "fit" and has a good laugh over the language issues. When she laughs, she glows.

*   *   *

Maris felt as though he was losing his wife. Now he would be working during the week, and on weekends, his wife and children would be leaving him. He was deeply wounded and didn't understand what Inguna was doing.

"I cried, but I took my children, and we went to DTS that summer anyway."

It was the first time she had heard the basics of Christianity. She and the other eighty people knew nothing of God. But that summer, several things happened that would affect Inguna and thereby Latvia, me, and even you, the reader. People began praying for Elina, and she improved. She started flourishing—she got her life back again. Two years of Inguna watching her daughter fail to respond to anything, and now Elina was stirring. It was a breath of fresh air to this mother's broken heart.

One summer afternoon, with the sun upon her face, Inguna went back behind the school to a small garden. She was hemmed in by the building on one side and the forest on the other. It was quiet, and the green landscape ran over hills and small valleys all around. The ground didn't shake, and the sky didn't split open; but in that moment, she knew everything she had been learning was true. Her own future death was clear to her, and she knew she'd stand before God. She knew her only hope was Jesus, and that without him, she would be cast headlong into hell. No one would listen to her excuses then. No objection would suffice to stay the just hand of God.

In that instant, as the cool summer breeze stroked her hair and the sun warmed her face, God was talking to her heart. She knew she was a sinner; she knew she needed Jesus. She asked Jesus to save her. That afternoon in the garden, Inguna went from blind to seeing, dead to living, enemy to daughter of God. Though it seemed to be the beginning, the truth is that God had been preparing her for this moment for two years. This had been his plan, and he had unfolded it according to his wisdom and for his glory.

*　*　*

As Inguna retells how she came to meet Jesus, I can't help but smile. Of course, I have known all along her story was leading to this point, but I still feel a sense of victory and rejoicing as she speaks.

"I want to go there," I say. "I want to see the school and the garden. Will you take me?"

Inguna furrows her brow and thinks for just a second.

"Of course, of course." The words come quickly and curtly though I know there is no ill will in them. She jots a few notes of her own. "We will go tomorrow, and I will also show you where I grew up and the apartment we lived in when I met Joann." She scribbles a little more then asks, "Where do you and Ken want to eat lunch?"

From Persecutor to Preacher: Paul's Story

He used to be called Saul. He was born in Tarsus in Cilicia, but he was brought up in Jerusalem. His appetite for learning was evident as he sat at the feet of Gamaliel and was educated according to the strict manner of the law. No one could accuse him of being unrighteous in terms of the law, for he held to it blamelessly. Saul had become a religious leader in his community. He was a Pharisee and handled himself with the utmost discipline. He had never married but rather poured himself into his work. There was no Pharisee greater or more prominent.

Saul had witnessed, in and around Jerusalem, a teacher who swayed the crowd with relative ease. This Jesus spoke with conviction and authority all while displaying great power. It was impossible that he should go unnoticed. Though Jesus had been crucified and buried, his followers declared him resurrected. Saul was outraged by such obvious blasphemy. Jesus had declared himself equal with God, and that warranted death. Now the disciples of Jesus were stirring up trouble everywhere. Within weeks, thousands of people purported to be followers of this carpenter turned savior.

One such man went by the name of Stephen. He was full of grace and power, doing great wonders among all those who lived in the region. He was arrested—on false charges, of course. But even as the lies piled up on him, those present took note that his face was like an angel. When Stephen opened his mouth, he spoke with wisdom and beauty that could not be withstood, but his closing remarks were too much for the council. He set the death of the Righteous One squarely at their feet. The people in the crowd flew to rage and gnashed their teeth at him. Like children, they plugged their ears against his words and rushed at him with a loud cry. Like men turned beasts, a pack of wild wolves, they fell upon Stephen and stoned him to death. As men stepped forward to cast rocks at this heretical preacher, they laid their coats with care at the feet of Saul the Pharisee. He fully approved of this execution; blasphemers were to be put to death. Stephen looked to heaven as he fell to his knees and asked that God wouldn't hold this sin against these men who only thought they knew and served God. A flurry of stones fell heavy upon him as each of those gathered about scoured the ground for another projectile. With that, he breathed his last.

Saul had no compassion; no warmth stirred in his heart. Rather, a zealous fire was stoked, and he became resolute with single-minded focus. As the dust settled, the crowd dispersed, and the frenzy died down, Saul smiled wickedly. This was exactly what should happen to those who followed the blasphemer known as Jesus of Nazareth. Each one should be buried under a pile of stones and left bloody and broken. Saul stepped away from the scene with schemes and murder in his mind. He persecuted unto death those who held to the way of Jesus. With relish, he bound and delivered men and women over to prison. He was on his way to Damascus in order to pour out the full measure of his fury on any he should find who held fast to the testimony of Jesus. He breathed in hate and breathed out death. Little did he know that God had set him apart from the womb for proclaiming the gospel of salvation. It had never entered his mind that what he was doing was in direct opposition to the God who had fashioned him with such tender care. As he and his entourage made their way along the road, the sky shone with a great light. The suddenness of it and the forcefulness of it caused him to fall to the ground.

"Saul, Saul, why are you persecuting me?" The words echoed in his ears like thunder and shook him to the core, draining all color from his face.

"Who are you, Lord?" The words came from his mouth, but I imagine he felt small and mouselike in that moment.

"I am Jesus, whom you are persecuting. But rise and enter the city, and you will be told what you are to do."

Saul rose from the ground, his fellow travelers stunned to silence by the voice that spoke from the sky. Saul was blind. He had seen Jesus, and he would never be the same. The man who had marched with venom in his mouth was now being led by the hand to Damascus. The iron gaze had been broken, and the bloodstained hands had been washed clean. Nothing would ever be the same again.

Three days later, Ananias, a believer from Damascus, was instructed by Jesus to pray for Saul that he would regain his sight. Ananias was understandably hesitant.

"I have heard how much evil this man has done to your saints at Jerusalem."

It seemed a fair point. This man Saul had come to Damascus to make captives of those who worshiped Jesus. Ananias would have certainly been on that list. But then Jesus said again, "He is my chosen instrument and will carry my name before the Gentiles and kings and even the children of Israel. He will suffer much for the sake of my name."

Ananias went to the place where Saul had come to rest. What a thing it was to walk into the small house and see there the man who had come with the intent of arresting and probably killing him. Yet Ananias was a faithful man, and he went and laid his hands on this chosen instrument of God.

"Brother Saul"—the words seemed so peculiar to say and equally peculiar to hear—"the Lord Jesus who appeared to you on the road has sent me so you may regain your sight and be filled with the Holy Spirit."

In that very moment, the one who had been blind was able to see as scales fell from his eyes. The sight he gained in that breath of a moment wasn't just of earthly things; he now had fully come to understand the things of Jesus. The Scripture he had dedicated himself to knowing now he knew afresh in light of the wonderful son of God. The truth of salvation through Christ alone flooded his mind. He had come to know the living one! (See Acts 7–9; Acts 22; Phil. 3.)

When God Changes the Heart:
Our Story

I'm not sure what your story is like. Maybe like Inguna you were an atheist and didn't even give God a thought at all. Perhaps you were more like Paul, very religious but knowing nothing of Jesus. I was just a kid. I hadn't yet turned four, but my parents had me in church every week. I'd sit there in the evening service and do my best to listen. I'd fumble with the old hymnal or look at how blue the old ladies' hair seemed by the lights hanging high overhead. I found it boring mostly. But there was one night in February 1979 when questions were stirred inside me relating to death and sin and forgiveness through Jesus. I was riveted and a little worried. I couldn't wait to get home so I could better understand what the fat preacher had been talking about.

The four of us—my sister Haley was barely one—lived in the Ye Olde English Apartments. They were painted dark brown. A row of shrubs lined a sidewalk next to the street, and one could often find me there in my overalls following my windup helicopter along the walkway. The place was torn down a while ago and is a gas station now. It was the first home I remember.

It seemed late to me, but I was young, so it may have just as easily been seven o'clock. I poked my head into my mom's room and asked to talk. I don't remember the content of the conversation, but I will never forget its course as I crawled into bed with my mother that night to talk to her about God. She explained that those who put faith in Jesus would live with him forever in heaven. Heaven particularly appealed to me. I can't imagine that our conversation was too lengthy, but it ended with a prayer. A small boy begged that Jesus would wash away his sins. That was the night I was saved. I leapt from her bed and hastened to my dad, who was doing laundry in his burgundy underwear. That moment has been written indelibly on my mind.

I had, to that point, been just as blind as Inguna or Paul. To that point, my heart had already been stained enough by the sin inherited from Adam to be cast to hell forever. Truly, from the moment I had come into this world, I had been marked by sin for death. But now God had made me new. I had been rescued from my sin, and my guilt had been replaced by holiness. I knew it and believed it with every fiber of my being. A few weeks later, I stopped the pastor in the hallway of the church and enthusiastically proclaimed, "One day I will do what you do."

I couldn't tell you what he said, but he flashed me a big smile as he bent down on one knee to speak to me, and I felt unstoppable.

That was how my journey began—no drama, no heinous life of crime to cover up, just a boy in need of a Savior and the moment that Jesus changed my life.

Loved by the Church: Inguna's Story

April in Latvia was cooler than I had expected. Inguna and I sat in her office waiting on Ken to finish a phone call so we could go and explore some of the key places of her life and specifically see where she had come to know God. A few minutes passed, and we piled into her car and were off. The drive would take about an hour, and I pulled out my green moleskin to continue my notes. My mind was buzzing with all we had discussed the previous day. The questions came slower for me as I watched the landscape hurry past my window. I was lost in the beauty of everything around me and the story I had been recording.

"Ask some more questions. Isn't there more you want to know?" Ken chimed in from the backseat periodically. I smiled at his excitement. He was thrilled to be here in this moment, thrilled about the book, thrilled about Inguna and her ministry. You could see the passion for this ministry in his eyes, and his bearded face did little to disguise his eager smile.

"I'm processing it all," I responded with a chuckle. In my head, I could already see the story coming together, and I was excited and terrified at the same time. We pulled up to the place the discipleship program had met all those years ago and got out of the car.

The main building serves as a hospital of sorts now, but I didn't see another soul. The place was tranquil and felt isolated. It seemed that perhaps it had been vacated for our visit so we could just enjoy the moment together. I imagined that someone might look out of the second-story window and watch us walk around taking pictures, wondering why we had come. Or maybe we weren't noticed at all. Perhaps not an eye fell on us as we walked among the trees and in and out of shadows. Maybe no one cared. There were a few buildings scattered around the piece of land, and trees towered on all sides. A mound of earth was off to my left with a wooden door set in its side. A tiny log cabin sat just behind that. I inquired about the mound as I had noticed many of them on the drive, and though I was certain they weren't hobbit homes, I really had no idea what they might be. It turns out they were food cellars. I wanted to know more. I had one hundred questions related to Latvia and my surroundings, but that wasn't why I had come, so my mind turned to other things.

Inguna walked me back to the garden where she had first become a Christian, and we stood there with the cold wind boxing our ears and leaving them red. All traces of a garden were gone. Large logs had been arranged for sitting. The moment wasn't deeply profound, but it did give me pause to reflect again on the small apartment where I had come to know the Lord. That was the place everything changed for me, and here I was standing on the ground where Inguna had met Jesus. I know it isn't the place where we meet Christ that matters but rather that we have met him. Still, I was delighted to be there. I had been invited into her story for that moment. She posed for a picture. She had exchanged her trademark purple for black leather boots that struck her just below the knee, black jeans, and a black down-filled coat. A turquoise scarf hung about her neck, giving a snap of color, and her raven hair framed her beaming smile and oversized sunglasses. She really was quite infectious. She was also all business.

"So in that afternoon in the garden behind the school, I invited Jesus into my heart—I realized I was a sinner. Peace instantly grew in my heart. I knew my child wasn't going to die at six years old, but then a new fear came in. This precious child of mine was going to live, but what kind of life would it be? She wouldn't have real friends and wouldn't be able to enjoy real life, would she? Then I remembered the prayer I had prayed in that old Lutheran church." With that, I was transported back to the younger version of Inguna and the story that had captured my attention and affection.

"I sat there in the garden, a brand new person in Christ, and I remembered that I had promised God that if he would save my child's life, then I would serve him." God had spared Elina just as Inguna had asked. However, a horrible thought struck her as she sat in the garden, and she blazed with anger at herself from two years gone by. Why hadn't she prayed that her daughter would be healed? Why had she only prayed that she would live? She felt guilt and shame wondering if her daughter's handicap was due to her lack of faith. The summer sun beat down on her face as she sat there in that garden. God had done what she had asked even though she had been a stranger to him. He had shown her compassion and kindness in these two years, and her daughter had just begun to show signs of vigor and joy again after so long. Now she had to fulfill her promise to him. But what would that look like? What could she possibly do to serve God? She was quite new to knowing about him and only minutes into actually knowing him as Savior.

Then it came to her. She needed to start a school. It exploded inside her like fireworks. The idea had been waiting there like a seed in fresh soil. God had planted it long ago, and now the Spirit within her caused it to spring to life. She would start a school where healthy or handicapped children could learn about God. Solid academics were a must, but most importantly, they'd be given an opportunity to learn about Jesus. Her Soviet upbringing weighed heavily on her mind; she had been taught, after all, that handicapped people were second-class citizens to be tucked away out of the public eye. Growing up, she had never even been aware there were handicapped people in her community, but now she was a different sort of person. Now she knew Christ. Things were different than they had been just moments ago. How unfair it was to think that those with handicaps should be put out of sight and mind.

"I knew it was unfair because the soul of my child was not handicapped. And one day, God will give my daughter a new body."

*　　*　　*

The statement left Inguna's mouth and struck me deeply. I had met Elina earlier in the week. She was working at the school along with her mother. Her joy was abundantly obvious, and she spoke of Jesus with such plainness and simplicity, like a child speaks of knowing her mother or favorite toy. Elina had given me a tour of the entire complex and didn't leave out a single coat closet or picture on the wall. She boasted in the work that was happening there and bragged on the graciousness of those who had come to serve or had simply given their money to the continued work of Talsi Christian School. I met every teacher, and we interrupted every class. It was the most thorough tour

I'm ever likely to receive. As Inguna spoke about that day in the garden twenty-two years earlier, as she spoke of her daughter, whose soul was not crippled, my heart leapt within me. What Inguna had known twenty-two years earlier, I was witnessing now. Elina had a body she would one day trade in for an imperishable one, but her soul had already been made new by the profound work of Jesus. A myriad thoughts of God's saving power flooded my mind as my pen drew arrows and exclamation points around that one line in my notes, "the soul of my child was not handicapped," but Inguna didn't pause for my moment of reflection.

*   *   *

"The ultimate goal would be to teach children about God. Until the 1940s, we had a godly heritage as a country, but for fifty years, we had been molded into an atheistic and communist community. Christianity was wiped out. Pastors had been exiled to Siberia. But when God gives you a vision, he provides. I tell you all this today, but back then, it wasn't that easy."

Inguna finished out the summer program in 1992 and continued to go to church, though it carried more weight for her than before. Though she was growing in her faith, things at home were more difficult than ever.

One night as she and Maris sat in their tiny Soviet kitchen, Inguna began sharing Jesus with her husband. Maris listened quietly, but the rage on his face was obvious. Finally, he fixed his eyes on Inguna.

"Tell me honestly," he demanded. "Who do you love the most, me or God?"

Inguna paused, knowing full well what was coming, before answering, "Honey, I know you will not understand me, but I love God the most." She could see the hurt in his expression, and his eyes seemed to go dark, so she quickly added, "But God gives me love to love you, our children, and other people."

Maris stood up quietly and somehow was more imposing than he had ever been. His voice didn't shake as he spoke but was overflowing with contempt. "Thank you, Inguna. It was all I had to know." From that moment, their lives would scarcely intersect.

At least at church, Inguna had some friends. Her coworker Verners attended the same church and was quite welcoming to her. They had become friends, and the book that had previously offended her as one with "blood dropping" out of it had become part of her life, albeit a minor one for the time being. In the coming months, she would be flooded with love for the Scripture.

One day, Verners beckoned her over to meet a man named Maris Dzelzs. Maris was a father of four and worked with Youth with a Mission. He had mentioned that Talsi needed a Christian school.

Verners turned to him, smiling, and said, "Maris, I'd like you to meet Inguna, the principal of Talsi Christian School."

Inguna laughed it off, but God had already begun to develop in her heart the ministry he had in store for her, and Verners had just served as a prophet of what was yet to come. It was December, and the promise she had made to God that summer of starting a school seemed far off and unlikely. Inguna continued with her life as many of us do when God has cast a vision for us and the way before us seems tenuous. She didn't have the slightest idea where to begin, so the idea lay dormant at best and stagnant at worst.

One evening, she shared with Maris the idea of beginning a school. She knew it was risky to bring him in on her dreams. His voice had nothing soft about it as he spoke.

"Now, Inguna, you listen, and you listen good! Once you told me you love God the most. I don't see this God in my kitchen, so I can take that. When you open a Christian school, it will be in the second place in your life. Our children will be in the third. Finally, your books and hobbies will come, and I will be in the fifth or sixth place in your life. I don't need that. If you open a Christian school, I will divorce you."

The words were difficult for Inguna to process, and before she could respond, he left the kitchen and slammed the front door as he disappeared into the night air. Inguna felt her soul crash within her. Tears streamed down her face as she hurried to their bedroom and flung herself upon the floor.

"God! Help! Whatever decision my husband makes will be his own, but I will open the Christian school."

Winter melted into spring, which found its way to summer, and before long, Inguna was once again at the discipleship training school with daughters in tow. Zane was six, and Elina was four. One of the guest teachers for a week that August was a man named John. He was from Tyler, Texas, and was headed to South Africa to do further mission work. They became quick friends, and Inguna confided in him concerning the school she was convinced she should start but had done nothing with for the last year.

"I have no education, and I don't even know the difference between Christian and secular school," she admitted.

John informed Inguna there was a teacher training program in Tyler for those who wanted to know and teach the Bible, but it seemed impossible to her that she would even be able to make it to America. Later in the week, a small prayer meeting took place at Maris Dzelzs's house to seek the Lord and his will for Inguna as it related to moving to Texas for training. Maris boldly put her on the spot.

"You will pray out loud and with English," he stated.

Inguna shook. It would be the first time she had ever prayed in public. She was a believer, but she still felt small and unequipped. She looked at the faces in the room, and embarrassment swept over her. She knew they would be able to tell she wasn't good at praying, that she was inept. Her heart raced, and her thoughts rushed like a torrent through her mind. She cared so deeply what these people would think of her. But no one mocked or laughed. In fact, they each genuinely loved her and were eager to see what God was going to do in and through her. Before John left for Africa, he asked her if she knew anyone in America. She recalled September 1991 and Joann.

"I know one person," she nodded. Two years earlier, as Joann said good-bye, she shoved a piece of paper with her phone number on it into Inguna's hand. At the time, Inguna thought it was ridiculous that Joann would give her a phone number. She was never going to see this woman again; why in the world would she need to call a woman from Texas? But she had kept the number for nearly two years, and now she was passing on this scrap of paper to John. With that, he was off to Africa.

School started a few weeks later, and she was back to work. Inguna let her boss know she may be moving to America. Though she had asked her principal to keep it private, the news became known quickly, and jealousy was stirred up among her coworkers. However, as each day passed, it seemed more unlikely that she would be able to go to Texas; classes there had already started, and there wasn't any money available for such a trip. She didn't even know if John had ever contacted Joann or if John even remembered her once he made it to his next destination.

Inguna wasn't in the daily habit of reading the Bible yet, but God pressed a verse into her mind that she knew she had to read: "As for you, son of man, prepare for yourself an exile's baggage, and go into exile by day in their sight" (Ezek. 12:3). She took it as a sign God was preparing to move her family to Texas and was flushed with fresh encouragement. On the first of October, Maris and Inguna acquired four visas so they could travel to the land of opportunity. Maris was excited about going to America and living what he imagined to be an abundant life. So the family waited. As Inguna recalled, they had their "visas and a promise from God."

John had in fact reached Joann and had asked her to help Inguna get to Tyler. Joann raised all the support necessary to bring Inguna to Texas though it wasn't easy. Since finances were tight, she told Inguna it might not be the time to come, but Joann asked how much Inguna needed and went again to her Sunday school class asking for help. A gentleman named Brent Cooper wrote a check for a thousand dollars to cover the remainder of the need, and the tickets were sent to Latvia. However, when the airline tickets arrived, there were only three. The church simply did not have the means to bring all four over at this time. Maris would have to stay behind. He was angry and hurt. His wife was set to leave him and take their children with her. He felt betrayed and rejected. Inguna knew she needed to go and promised to get money together to bring Maris over as soon as she was able, but Maris was not convinced. He accused Inguna of loving Jesus and Christianity more than she loved him. Inguna did love Maris very deeply, but she knew she had to obey what God had put before her. Inguna and the girls left their husband and father and headed to Texas while a bevy of emotions swirled in them all.

The trip was a long one, made more so by the young girls at her side and the growing mixture of excitement and nervousness that rested in the pit of her stomach. There is little like the feeling of walking into a new place where one is unknown and unknowing. We've each felt it at some point—when going to kindergarten or leaving home for the first time to go to college—but it is wildly different when arriving in a new culture among a new people entirely. English was not Inguna's first language, and her husband was far away. She sat in the car being shuttled to her new home in Tyler. Exhaustion pulled on her eyelids, and uneasiness was heavy on her heart.

They finally pulled up to a trailer home on the small Youth with a Mission campus. It seemed nice enough from the outside. Her hosts had brought their teen daughter along with them, and they all ushered the weary travelers inside. The first thing Inguna noticed was the teen trying to smash a big bug with her shoe, and a moment of panic set in. To what type of place had she come? What was she doing here? But a second look reassured her. There wasn't much to the trailer; it had a stove, beds, and a microwave. Inguna stood there with her luggage and her little girls in the middle of an empty living area. No chairs, no table, nothing; but it was still the nicest place she had ever lived in. This was going to be home.

Inguna took to her classes with vigor. She was an eager student dedicated to using her time well. She would contact Maris and let him know she was working on getting the money to bring him over as soon as she could.

Meanwhile, the little family was working to make the trailer feel like home. During the week, she and her girls would eat lunch at the teacher training facility. The rest of the time, they made due at the local food bank. Boxes of macaroni and cheese and cans of green beans filled the cabinet. It could hardly be called plentiful, but it was sufficient; though to this day, Inguna still wrinkles her nose and screws up her face at the idea of ever eating pasta or preserved green beans again. She still calls to mind the first time that a woman named Barbara took her and the girls to a grocery store. The size of the place and the overflowing shelves left her speechless. At home they had been limited by the government to a pound of meat and a pound of butter per week. Barbara indicated that Inguna should grab a shopping cart. Inguna was so grateful for her friend's kindness, but wanting to be polite, she was determined to buy only the cheapest items she could find. She hadn't had meat in weeks, so she began to consider her options. There to the side of the steak, roast, chicken, and pork were some pig's feet. The packages looked like presents to Inguna with their yellow Styrofoam tray and the transparent plastic. Two packages should do it. She had grown up eating pig's feet, and this was going to be a great feast for the small family that had been barely getting by.

A month after arriving in Texas, Joann's father used his free airline miles to bring Maris to Texas. It was a happy reunion for the couple—but only for a moment. In Latvia, Maris was an engineer; but in the States, with only a student visa and a language barrier, he wasn't able to work. He was frustrated by his circumstances and felt humiliated and degraded.

*   *   *

On that cold December day when Inguna and I first met as Wayne was driving us to Brent's office, I had asked about her husband, Maris. I had wondered if he had come to Christ when she had, if he had been as excited about starting a school. She let me know that it was a slower process for him.

"How did your husband come to know the Lord then?" I'd asked.

Her face beamed from the back seat of the car, and her eyes moistened. She cocked her head to the side and pursed her lips together. Then she spoke a single word. "Love." She nodded slightly as if to say, "Isn't it always love that brings us to Jesus?" I knew in that moment that I would be writing the book you are reading now.

* * *

The family had been attending Green Acres Baptist Church and had already plugged in to a Sunday school. Maris wouldn't speak because he felt unsure of his English and was a devout perfectionist. The family felt a little out of place, but the people there were genuinely loving and caring to them. One day, after the service ended, Pastor David stopped Maris and Inguna.

"We are having a baptism service in a couple of weeks, Inguna, and I was wondering if you would like to be baptized," the pastor asked. Inguna was excited for the opportunity as it was still something she had not done. "Maris, we could baptize you too," the pastor said. Inguna is certain the pastor knew Maris still wasn't a believer and believed he was creating an opportunity to open the dialogue.

"That would make me a Baptist, then?" Maris answered in broken English. "I suppose I couldn't have a beer and watch the football game anymore?"

"It isn't about the beer," Pastor David responded with a smile. "It's about knowing Jesus, and as you come to know him better, you will find that the things you used to do don't appeal to you as much as they used to."

God was doing a work within Maris, and he already had been won over, especially when he saw how well his daughters were treated by those around him. He had never seen such love from people before. It was so unconditional and honest. The following week, he gave his life to Jesus, and a week after that, he was baptized. From that moment forward, it was no longer just Inguna who had a heart to honor God with a Christian school; her husband's heart now beat in tune with hers. More importantly, her husband finally shared her love of Jesus. It was December 1993.

"My dream was just to go to the States and see the land of opportunity," Maris said of that time in his life. "The people in my class showed me the love of Jesus, and that broke my heart the most. One evening, I asked God, Can he save me? Can my sins be forgiven? Since that moment, God has changed my life."

A few months later, in early February, Inguna and Maris were at a prayer meeting with their Sunday school teacher, Roy. Roy had been such an encouragement to them. He had grown fond of them as well and said, "When you leave, I will sneak home as your third child."

Inguna laughed and asked, "How about as my fourth child?"

Roy stared, wide-eyed. "Are you pregnant?"

"I don't know," Inguna answered softly. Maris and Inguna had been given bad information when Elina first went to the hospital three and a half years earlier. They had been told that a cyst from Inguna had gone into Elina's body when she had been developing. The doctors had told Inguna that all their daughter's ailments were Inguna's fault. This had so terrified the young couple that they had decided to have no more children. But as God would have it, they were expecting baby number 3.

The pregnancy proved to be a turning point for the growing family. The class rejoiced with them at the news, but it hadn't been until that very moment that anyone in the class knew the conditions in which Maris and Inguna had been living. From then on, every week, a different family from the class provided bags of groceries for their adopted Latvian friends.

"They blessed us. They didn't allow us to feel like beggars. Rather, they let us know they were blessed with the opportunity to serve," Inguna said. She felt their deep love.

After more than four months of boxed pasta and canned green beans, the cupboards finally did run over. One Sunday after church, several families offered to buy Maris, Inguna, and the girls lunch. They went to Pauline's Country Buffet. It was the first time any of them had ever been to a buffet before, and they couldn't believe the sheer volume of food available to them. Anything they could have wanted was there for the taking, and if they made a bad gamble and decided the casserole or the pink stuff wasn't to their liking, they could simply set that plate aside and start all over.

"What kind of drink do you want?" asked a friend. Just the idea that there were choices overwhelmed the couple. Never had they experienced such opulence. Never had they experienced such friendship. Trips to Dairy Queen for Blizzards and pickup games of volleyball became a regular part of their lives. While Inguna loved the Blizzards—particularly the Tropical Blizzard with extra pecans—Maris was in love with volleyball; he was, after all, an athlete.

One night, as the ball came over the net, Maris spoke his first public word in English: "Block!" he shouted. He had finally found his place in Texas. He finally felt safe. It wasn't much longer before the Sunday school class had talked Green Acres Baptist into hiring Maris to help with maintenance. Once again, he was employed. Roy would also call Maris any time he had an odd job around the house. The kids were happy; Maris and Inguna were happy. Life was good.

*   *   *

Inguna smiles at me as she recalls the way the church cared for her family all those years ago—even in the little details.

"I had never had anyone show me how to wear my makeup. I wore very bright cosmetics. I didn't know." She waves her hand around as she speaks and breaks into a small laugh. "I'm sure it was horrible. But there was a woman in our class who came to me one day and said she wanted to help me with my makeup. Her daughter was a cosmetic specialist, and we were going to have a women's party. She put it to me so nicely that my makeup needed to be changed. I couldn't have even had it in my mind to be offended. So we had a party at her house, and her daughter did my makeup. They gave me so much makeup. She had the expensive stuff." Inguna speaks so fondly of her friends from church. Now twenty years gone by, I can't help but think about the many people who cared for me along the way. It was clear she wouldn't be the woman sitting across from me today if not for those foundational friendships.

*   *   *

None of these things were overwhelming for the small class. A bag of groceries here and a Blizzard there, perhaps another trip to the buffet—such small acts didn't even constitute sacrifices. But for Maris and Inguna, it was precisely these small things that warmed their hearts and made them feel included. This was the love that won them over.

God's People Loved Well: Paul's Story

Paul wasn't ever one to sit quietly and contemplate what he should do next. He was passionate and ambitious. No one would accuse him of taking things slowly. But three days of blindness had tempered him a little—only a little. Encountering Jesus on the road had altered the trajectory of his life, and he found himself in a small room looking into the face of Ananias, essentially a stranger but also now a brother, a friend. He spent the next few days with the disciples in Damascus. Paul ate bread with those he had intended to bring to trial. How profound it must have been when Ananias first escorted Paul into a living room where a table was set with food. Ananias must have mentioned who Paul was; he had to have told them of the encounter with Jesus and the change in this man. He who had formerly been their enemy was instantaneously their friend. What a shock it must have been for Paul when the lady of the house brought a bowl of water for his feet and treated him as a favored guest. How unsettling it must have been to look into the smiling bearded face of a man who just passed him a piece of bread or fish and to think, *I was going to throw this man in jail and would have gladly cast my vote in favor of his execution.*

Though it must have been humbling and inspiring to Paul, it was certainly nothing new for those who had been faithfully following Jesus. They knew no other thing than to love this man just as Jesus loved him, and they did that well. The very ones he had planned harm against were now embracing him with the love and grace that comes from knowing God. It wasn't the believers in Damascus who had a problem with Paul as he boldly and faithfully proved from the Scripture that Jesus was the Messiah; it was the unbelieving Jews who sought to put Paul to death. Paul was awash in the love of those he had three days earlier hated with the utmost hatred. Three days ago, he had been convinced he was doing God a service by wiping out these so-called heretics. Now everything had changed. Love had changed it.

Paul was an educated man—certainly more educated than those playing host to him. So it didn't take long before Paul began preaching in Damascus, nor did it surprise anyone when he took to it with great ease. He knew the Scripture so well and was able to prove so thoroughly that Jesus was the Christ that Paul even amassed some disciples of his own. The people were likely thrilled to have such a one as Paul teaching and preaching the truth of the cross.

Of course, not all were thrilled; and somewhere in secret, men came together with a vile purpose. They couldn't let this Pharisee-turned-follower of Jesus remain alive. He was causing the whole city to be stirred up in favor of this Christ.

The anger Paul felt earlier toward the believers was now felt toward him. News was carried by God's gracious provision to Paul's disciples that his life was being hunted. They pleaded with Paul to flee for his life so he might continue to faithfully proclaim the gospel. And so, under the cover of darkness and with a rope and a basket, the disciples gathered to lower Paul down the city wall. The gates would certainly be guarded; it seemed there was nothing better to do. The basket was secured to the rope and pushed out the window. Paul stepped to the sill and tested the basket with one foot and then the other. It seemed secure enough. The basket groaned and creaked as the wicker sagged and flexed beneath the strain of a full-grown man.

"Go slowly, men."

Hand over hand, the disciples gave a little rope, and they watched Paul sink away into the darkness of night. In the quiet, it seemed to take so long for the basket to reach the ground. The only sound was the gentle whirring of the rope as it slid across the window ledge and down the wall into the abyss. Then the rope went slack. Paul had touched down. The basket was pulled back to the window.

The preacher was gone; they prayed he was safely away and that they would see him again.

Paul could just barely make out the light in the window through which he had just descended. He ran from the wall into the night, feeling his way along rocky paths and grassy hills. This life was going to be different than the one he had known as a Pharisee. In time, Paul found himself in Jerusalem. He longed so deeply to join the disciples, but unlike those in Damascus, there had not been an Ananias to appeal to the brethren on his behalf. So he found the believers wary and fearful, still believing Paul to be a murderer at heart. However, the change in Paul hadn't gone unnoticed by everyone; and Barnabas, a faithful follower of Jesus, brought Paul to the apostles and declared to them how Christ had spoken to Paul and how Paul had even faithfully preached Jesus in Damascus. From that point forward, there was none who belonged to Jesus who wouldn't receive Paul, and he went in and out among them in exuberance and joy, preaching boldly in the name of the Lord.

Paul was loved and cared for by those among whom he preached. Certainly, on his many missionary trips, his life was in grave danger, but he was ever adored by the church in each place he found himself. So much was he loved by the Galatians when he first came to that region in physical ailment, they neither despised him nor scorned him to shame but would have given him their own eyes if possible. They received him as an angel of God. The Macedonian church in its extreme poverty sought not only to meet Paul's needs but to meet the needs of those who were serving the Lord well in Jerusalem.

The love of Christ had redeemed him. His love for Christ engaged him, and the love he received from the brethren upheld and enabled him to carry on the work of God. God is love and that love was working in and through Paul now.

Shaped by the Body of Christ: Our Story

I have come to be the man I am today—a husband, father, and pastor—because of the way those in the body of Christ loved and cared for me. Inguna and Paul were both advanced by the gracious care of God through his church, and we find that even in our very normal lives, that truth still resounds in our hearts.

I had been a Christian since I was three, but the idea of discipleship was foreign to me.

At twelve, there was a woman who taught a class for our youth on how to share our faith. Only the pastor's daughter and I went to the class. I can't remember the woman's name, but for a year, she loved us and taught us well. She was a friend to us.

At sixteen, I was getting up early on Thursday and going to a men's Bible study at the church I attended. There were about eight men there, and we were going through the book of Mark. I still remember our conversation on chapter 2. At school there was a guy named Erin. He was (and continues to be) godly. He loved the Lord but was also very popular—something I still haven't achieved. He would meet me at the church. Those older men and Erin all just loved me well. They inspired me to a deeper love of Jesus.

John Strappazon was my college pastor, and he discipled a group of us for three or four years in a row. His heart for discipleship was unmatched. He believed—rightly so—that real disciples should always be training others to make disciples. What he taught me then continues to resonate in my heart today. That was about the same time Inguna was arriving in Tyler. All of us are still serving the Lord.

Steve was a pastoral counselor I saw for a couple of years. He had a great smile and thick square glasses. He would weep for me when my heart was too hurt and angry to weep for myself. I remember mocking him for crying on my behalf. In the midst of brokenness and tears and piles of self-loathing, he faithfully pointed me back to sufficiency in Christ. I loved him, and he loved me well.

Jon Randles took me to IHOP. Over pancakes, he helped me to understand how ministry should look. He encouraged me and even gave me my first real opportunity to preach.

"Next week, before I preach, you get to have the first five minutes," he said.

I'll never forget the pressure I felt as I prepared for that sermon. I preached for four and a half minutes on worship.

When I finished, Jon told me, "You did a really great job. Next time I'll give you ten minutes." He continues to be a part of my life.

Scott, Ryan, and Roger were three of the best friends I could have wanted in my college years. Until I met them, I really did spend most of my time feeling isolated. They were more dynamic than I was and were certainly happier people than I had been at that point. We took annual fishing trips, prayed together, and studied the Scripture together. In general, we just did life with one another. It is largely because of something Scott once said to me that I am a preacher today. Scott and I met for two hours every Thursday night at our church's prayer chapel. For two years, we prayed together. For many years after that, we studied the Scripture together.

Mike and Tomi welcomed me into their home. They fed me and taught me. They bestowed more grace upon me than I had ever received and rebuked me with necessary kindness. To this day, I think on them fondly and credit them with shaping much of my twenties.

Jed had attended a college retreat at which I had preached in September 1999. The following Tuesday, at a midweek Bible study, he stopped me outside.

"I really enjoyed getting to know you this past weekend. I'd like to get together on a regular basis," he said.

I, too, had felt a connection to him and agreed we should start spending time together. The night was cold. He was in his incredibly cool glasses and dapper clothes, and I remember thinking he was a better dresser than I was. We spent the next two years studying the Bible together. Today he pastors a church in the Dallas area, and I still talk with him from time to time to get his input or advice on various situations. He is still a better dresser than I am.

Chris was my younger roommate who had a deep and flooding passion for the Word of God and an unbelievable knowledge of church history. Chris was a constant encouragement to me.

When I moved to a small community outside of San Antonio, it was Bill and Carol who adopted me into their home. For a full year, I ate dinner at their house every night. Their daughters became sisters to me, and I later officiated both of their weddings. Bill divided his small office in half and gave me a desk so I would have a place to study as I was getting my ministry started. For many years, they would hang a stocking for me along the staircase at Christmastime.

Lakan has been one of my most trusted counselors, teachers, and friends for the last ten years. There is seldom something that transpires in my life on which I don't seek his direction. Lakan has been a part of everything significant in my life, from officiating my wedding to the birth of my children to the day I decided to plant a church. I have never known a man so deeply in love with the Word of God and so overwhelmingly gracious to the people around him.

Micah has been my dear friend for more than twelve years. Hardly a week has gone by in those years where we have not sat down at least once and discussed Scripture. We preach together, pastor together, and study together, and we have grown immeasurably as we have challenged and encouraged one another. Aside from my wife, no one knows me so well or has influenced my spiritual life and ministry so deeply.

Ryan and I regularly grab lunch, and I'm grateful for his friendship and the constant biblical dialogue he offers.

Now many friends surround me, and I keep Tony, Lance, and Jason on speed dial. I could not have come to where I am in life and ministry without these faithful brothers who have loved me well through sorrow and sin. Isn't that the most beautiful form of love? They embraced me in my brokenness and my insecurity and loved me deeply. They saw past my foibles and the wars that waged within and lavished on me the gracious kindness of our God and redeemer. Most of them have seen my anger and my immaturity. Many of them have seen my tears and wounds. But all of them have loved me supremely.

You have your own list. I know you do. None of us has gotten to this place of trusting and knowing Christ without the love of others. There are those who champion us as we engage in the pugilistic conduct of living life. They have applied the balm of Jesus to our wounds. They have been the voices in our ears calling us to action when we felt our feet were too heavy to plod forward. They have held up our hands to do well the work God has set before us when we were certain we could not carry on. They have set under us the rock of Christ to overthrow our weakness with his almighty strength (Exod. 17:8–13). They have applauded our successes, never even realizing they emboldened us to complete the tasks at hand. Or perhaps they have emboldened us because they themselves were emboldened by others and have learned the value of love.

Tumultuous circumstances undoubtedly will clamber up our backs and rest again on our shoulders with heaviness. But if we can recall those who have—in obedience to Jesus—loved us well, we will find that once again we can hasten forward. They have wept with us and hurried to bear our burdens (Rom. 12:15; Gal. 6:2).

We aren't created to conduct solitary lives. We aren't saved to stand alone. When the church is behaving as it should, we find that it opens its loving arms and welcomes us in warm embrace. It is our love for one another that testifies to the world that we are truly disciples of Jesus (John 13:34–35).

Inguna and her family were overwhelmed by the love with which the church showered them. Maris came to believe in Jesus because of the great love cast upon his wife and his children. Those who have loved us well have facilitated our salvation and our growth. For most of us, we are mature and healthy people in Christ because a long line of people have cherished us as Jesus has.

We were never meant to be alone, and through the church, God has made sure we never shall be.

God's Glorious Provision: Inguna's Story

When Talsi Christian School officially started during the fall of 1995, there were thirty-seven students and eight staff. Monthly salary at the time was about eighty dollars per person. Tuition was only twenty dollars. For many years, government subsidies helped fund the school. But in recent years, the government help has been cut, and with more than 250 students and an annual budget of $800,000, there is a shortfall of nearly $12,000 a month.

"We pray and believe God will do more than we can even imagine or ask," Inguna answers when asked about her feelings regarding the current state of finances and provision for the school. "This is God's school. God holds the future of TCS. Of course, we would like to continue and to reach out to our community, Latvia, and beyond. God has always provided for us. We have been in difficult situations before with no other hope than to cry out to God."

Since the situation for Talsi Christian School is so dire, Ken and Brent came up with an idea to write a book in the hopes that all sales could help make up the deficit. They spoke to several publishers and several authors.

Each author fell by the wayside for one reason or another. Little did any of us know that God was working to provide exactly what it was each of us needed. Inguna would gain support, Ken and Brent would be able to facilitate that support, and through the project, I'd have some of my ministry needs met as well.

There we were in the car on the way to Brent's office. Wayne was driving, and Inguna was in the backseat bundled up. I had known Wayne for about two hours and Inguna for less than one. I was already hooked by Inguna's charm. We pulled into a parking garage.

"Now who is this we are going to meet with?" I asked.

"Brent Cooper," Wayne said.

I'd learn later that Brent had been supporting Inguna's ministry since before she came to Texas to study in 1993. He was the one who had written the check to provide the original plane tickets to America. We walked into a nice building in downtown Dallas and took the elevator to the second floor. I still wasn't sure what we were doing there. I just knew Ken had paid for my plane ticket, and he wanted me to meet Inguna and Brent. I also knew Wayne had been gracious enough to pick me up and drive me around for the day.

Out of the elevator and to the right, the center of the building opened with a view down to a nicely decorated part on the first floor. Another right turn led to the mammoth glass doors of a law firm with "Cooper" etched on the door. By the looks of the office, Brent Cooper appeared to be a lawyer who was good at his job. I felt out of place; my ratty tennis shoes that should have been replaced six months prior and my worn-out hoodie covered up by an old black leather coat made me look more like I should have been walking into a bowling alley rather than a swanky law firm. Wayne let the secretary know we were there to meet Brent, and she informed us he would be with us shortly. Wayne and Inguna talked about Brent and Ken, and my thoughts swam vicious circles in my brain.

Then there he was, Brent Cooper. I shook his hand and introduced myself. He had a pen and legal pad in hand. He was shorter than me but certainly more dignified and regal.

"Let's go down to this conference room and talk," he said politely.

The four of us sat down. Brent placed his back to the door and sat at the head of the table. Inguna was on his left. I sat directly across from her on Brent's right, and Wayne sat next to me. I was glad he sat next to me. I think I would have felt more nervous if they had all sat across from me. Brent is perhaps more business than Inguna, and we dove straight in

"So what are you thinking about the book?" Brent asked.

I must have looked foolish as I stammered. A week earlier, I couldn't have even pointed out Latvia on a map, and I'd only known this dark-haired boisterous Inguna for about an hour.

"Well, it really sounds interesting. I'm certainly wanting to learn more about the project," I said.

Brent himself is an accomplished author. Several of his books are used in law schools throughout Texas, and he has published dozens of articles in law journals. He struck me as being in his early-to-midsixties. His hair was gray and neatly trimmed, and though he was in slacks and a nice shirt, he didn't seem as distant as I had expected him to be. His eyes were crisp and sharp and keenly focused on whatever it was they met. His short gray moustache and goatee gave him a dignified look. He spoke very quickly; something urgent had come up, and he only had a few minutes to talk with us, but I had the feeling he was always in a hurry. He jotted notes on the legal pad of all we discussed, and I felt for a small moment like perhaps he was preparing to cross-examine me, but his friendly nature and easy conversation soon won me over.

"So we want this book to help meet some of the financial need for Inguna and Talsi Christian School," Brent said.

I can't even tell you now how it was he spoke with dignity and depth. Sometimes you are just in the presence of an educated individual, and you know it when he speaks. I'm not precisely sure how long we talked. He shared with me his ideas for the project and the direction he felt it should go.

"What direction do you think you'd take the book?" he asked.

It was a hard question because I knew so little information. Ken had called me five days earlier and told me he wanted people in churches today to see God was still active, so that's where I began.

"If the purpose of this book is that we would use it to help people see the God of Acts isn't gone but that he is still working, and if we want to use Inguna as a jumping-off place, then I think we need to tell a little bit of her story and show how it relates to the stories of the Bible. Then we can connect it to us. I'm afraid if it is too much of a biography, people may read it and think it a nice story but miss the connection it has to them." I didn't have anything else to say. I didn't know any more than that.

"Yes, yes!" Inguna's eyes lit up. "It must have the Bible in it. We must show that what God was doing he is still doing."

Though I'm sure the meeting had other ideas exchanged, I can recall very few of them. I gave Brent some of my books as Ken had requested. He wanted Brent to see my writing style. I felt small and sheepish in that moment, very much like a child. My books are all self-published. I can barely get them read by my friends, and here, these men were asking me to write a book to help facilitate the future ministry of a Christian school around the world. Brent hurried out of the office with his legal pad and my books on his way to the matter that was most pressing. I remember thinking how nice and warm he had been, and though I had felt insecurities swell within me when we first met, I was at ease by the time the meeting was over.

I asked Inguna to pose for a picture with me, which she graciously agreed to. Then Wayne, Inguna, and I were off for a quick bite of lunch. I was just beginning to get a feel for the ministry in Latvia and for the men who had been a part of it for so long. Brent had been serving Talsi Christian School for more than twenty years, Ken had been along for the ride the last twelve or so, and Wayne was the newest in this particular group. They all loved the school and the work being done there so much. Each had given time and money, each had bent the knee in prayer, and here they were again seeking ways to make sure the school would be kept running for years to come.

Inguna sat at lunch, confident and funny. She knew God would provide for the school. She didn't blink at it. Her surety was obvious. Her eyes sparkled. Her face beamed. Her back was straight, and her shoulders were square, with her chin tipped ever so slightly upward. This wasn't a beaten woman—she wasn't fearful or wringing her hands. She knew who God was. The things he had already done in her life and family informed how she felt about the future. Her only complaint in that moment was the previous day; Dairy Queen had been out of bananas and was therefore unable to make her favorite Blizzard. She wanted just one more before she returned to Latvia the following day. Though I could share this story with you, the humor of it is completely lost without her thick accent. I promise you, though, that should you and I ever cross paths, I will do my best Inguna impression and tell you about the Blizzard that wasn't.

It was 1994. Inguna was continuing her studies. Maris was working and happy. The girls were thriving, and the baby was developing. It was a very busy time. Elina wasn't completely well, and a doctor had suggested they buy some inexpensive braces for Elina's little legs; the gravity of their situation weighed them down.

"It couldn't have been more than ten dollars, but we had nothing," Inguna recalled. "We prayed God would provide for our little girl. Later that day, I checked our post office box, and we had a note there with a check for twenty dollars. God was always doing things like that. He always gave us what we needed."

As Inguna's pregnancy progressed, she wasn't sure how she would see a doctor. They didn't have any insurance, and their money was scarce, but members of their class led them to a doctor with a private practice out of a small home. On her first visit, she was heartbroken to find that the clientele were stinky and dirty. Maybe they were homeless. Maybe they were just down on their luck. Inguna couldn't help but think that moving to Texas in obedience to God had somehow moved her family to a lower class. Was this all her fault?

But when her turn to see the doctor came, he walked into the patient room with a smile. He was kind and caring. It was clear he wanted to make sure his patients were loved and treated well. Here was a doctor who didn't see dirty, stinking people or poor Latvian parents. He saw people— just normal people who needed help.

In May, her schooling came to an end, but Inguna's work in the States had not. However, it meant her family was no longer able to stay in the trailer on campus. But God would not let this family go homeless. Green Acres Baptist Church had a retreat property by the lake, and Pastor David had a cabin there they were allowed to live in. It was a beautiful place surrounded by trees, and the nightly choir of crickets and cicadas sang them to sleep. This would be home until the baby arrived.

About this time, Inguna began to visit churches on Sunday mornings, sharing the vision for Talsi Christian School and seeking financial support. The school didn't have land, a building, staff, or students, but it would. It would start its first year in September the following year and needed money to get things rolling. One Sunday early in August, the visitation process took Inguna and her family to FBC Dallas. The church members were very gracious to Inguna and her family; no sooner had they heard her report than they committed one hundred dollars a month to the formation and well-being of the school. That would have been it if not for Orville Rogers. The man was well into his seventies. He was a dapper dresser and stood to address those who had been gathered in the meeting. Silver hair topped his head, and his body trembled ever so slightly with age. He braced himself and spoke in a voice that seemed stronger than the body from which it came.

"We should vote for a thousand dollars a month," he stated. He didn't really need to say much more than that, and so he took his seat again. He was a patriarch of sorts, and his words carried great authority.

Those present were pricked to the heart as they exchanged glances and nodded their heads gently. There was another vote, and the church agreed that a thousand dollars per month should be the gift given. Inguna was elated. She had no idea whether that was a lot of money, but it felt like a true victory for her. This had been the largest gift she had received, and she knew the school was truly going to move forward.

By the time the summer came to an end, Inguna was quite pregnant. The thoughts of how they would pay for the hospital bill when it came time for delivery pressed upon the young couple. One afternoon, Roy and Martha—Roy's wife, who Inguna swears is an angel—took Maris and Inguna to an open house for the newly remodeled delivery department at Tyler East Texas Medical Center. He showed her the labor and delivery rooms and walked her through the halls. While Inguna and Maris took in the rest of the sights, Roy and Martha were talking to the director for the new medical center. Before long, Roy had convinced the director that it would be great publicity and a wonderful public relations story to deliver Inguna's baby for free.

That September, Inguna's son Janis was born. They named him Janis (John) because while she had been at the discipleship training program in Latvia the summer before, she had read of God's promise to Zechariah concerning the son he was to have named John. Inguna had underlined those verses in the opening chapter of Luke and had considered them a promise to her as well. The delivery went smoothly, and the staff was kind, but Inguna still laughs about how they left the hospital as quickly as the doctors would allow. Their family was now five strong, and the year in Texas had come to an end. It was time to return to Latvia, back to their home of Talsi, and it was time to build a school. Two weeks after Janis was born and shortly after Elina had received another brain surgery, which among other things also replaced the piece of missing skull bone, the family was off for its next adventure.

Maris and Inguna returned to their small two-room apartment but were fortunate enough also to buy the now-vacant one-room apartment adjacent to them. In January 1995, Roy came to help scout properties. Latvia is very far north, and January can be downright miserable, especially for those who can't afford heat. But Roy didn't complain once about the bitter nights. The Texas businessman and the Latvian mother met with the mayor to examine available buildings.

"I still remember walking in the snow around the old building with Roy," Inguna said "I thought the building was big enough since we were going to be such a small school."

The price for the building was fifty-two thousand dollars, and as it was Russian-owned, there was no negotiating. Talsi Christian School was now located right in the center of town. All that was left to do was recruit staff, get curriculum, find books, purchase equipment, and see if they could acquire any students.

That March, Inguna began to feel the pressure. They were only six months from the beginning of classes, and there was still much to do. Inguna asked her mother if she would be willing to keep Janis once school started. She and her mother were very close but had grown closer since Roy had visited in January; it was then that Inguna's mother had become a Christian. When Inguna first returned from the States, she shared the gospel with her mother and was surprised to hear her mother's story.

"Listen, Inguna," her mother had insisted. "I was ten when my mother died. As she lay on her death bed, she beckoned me to her and said, 'Vesma, if you believe in God, we will see each other in heaven again.' I will never forget that conversation, but it was the first mention I had ever heard her make of God."

Inguna's mother had carried the whisper of God for decades, but now he had rooted himself in her heart.

"I don't want to watch Janis," her mother replied to Inguna. "You know what, Inguna? I always want to be in school where I can implement my ideas. Would it be okay if I worked for you?" Inguna's first staff member was her mother. Vesma still serves there alongside her daughter even now.

That summer, Bill and Melanie Rogers made their way to Latvia to help see the school kicked off well. Bill was the son of Orville, who had helped get Inguna her first substantial donation, and Melanie was the director of a Christian school in Texas. Melanie had come to lead a teacher conference for the first eight teachers of Talsi Christian School (TCS). Summer gave way to fall, and in September 1995, TCS opened its doors. The dream had been realized.

The first big crisis came two years later at the beginning of the third year of classes. For each of the two previous years, Roy had come for the opening day of classes on September 1. However, this visit was a somber one: he was bringing news that there was no money and that the school would have to be closed because it couldn't pay the remaining balance on the building.

The students came in with joy on their faces and in an attitude of celebration, and Roy couldn't bring himself to break any hearts so he stepped outside to pray. Roy was begging God for help to understand. He wondered why, after having started the school, they were going to have to shut it down. As he prayed, a light fog was blowing along the ground and circling its way up to the bright red roof of the school. As the fog swirled and twisted, it formed unmistakably the word "faith." As clear as the nose on one's face, the fog spelled out "Faith"! Roy pulled a camera from his pocket and snapped a picture, and with that the word was gone. It was only 1997, so he would have to wait until the drugstore could develop it; but a few hours later, Roy shuffled through the pictures as quickly as he could. There it was: "faith" written on the red roof in the early morning haze.

*   *   *

"Do you still have that picture?" I asked. I tried not to break the rhythm of Inguna's vivid storytelling, but I wanted to see it.

"Yes, of course, of course" came her predictable reply. "I will find it tonight, and tomorrow when we drive out to the dicipleship school, I will show you."

The next morning, as we waited on Ken so we could hit the road, she handed me a worn photograph, faded by the last seventeen years. Yet there it was: the old school building, red roof, green trees towering around it, and right in the center, in wispy letters, "faith." Of course, the day before she had already told me the rest of the story of how God had provided for them and how the school was able to continue.

*   *   *

"Our final payment of ten thousand dollars was due that October, but we couldn't pay," she said. "In November, I called the Russians, and they gave me two weeks to pay or they were taking the building back. I had no idea how we could get so much money in such a short time."

As Inguna sat there in her small office, reflecting on the morning fog and the urgent need, an old, bent woman came in asking for the principal of the school. Inguna showed the woman into her office and offered her a chair. She was very small and poorly clothed and seemed quite frail. In her hand was a small plastic bag she clutched with her arthritic fingers.

"God told me to give you a donation," the woman said. The words hung in Inguna's ears, and she chuckled to herself wondering what sort of gift this poor old woman could give. She didn't even have decent clothes or a regular bag. Part of Inguna felt she didn't have time for this nonsense. This woman's ten dollars would be a pittance compared to the current need. But she forced a smile and thanked the woman as she held up the shoddy plastic bag. Inguna peered inside and gasped. There was a lot of money. Inguna felt ashamed.

"I can't take this much money from you. You need this."

"My son was in the USA on a monthlong student exchange program." The old woman smiled. "He recently visited a church, and as he was leaving, he shook the pastor's hand at the back door. It was a small church, and the pastor knew everyone who came. The kind pastor greeted my son and asked him where he was from. Of course, my son told him he was from Latvia. The pastor's eyes lit up, and he hurried my boy to his office and opened a safe. The pastor handed my son twenty thousand dollars and said, 'We had an old Latvian woman here for many years. When she died, she left this money to the church and asked that we return it to do ministry in Latvia, but I had no clue where Latvia even was. Could you please make sure this money gets used for ministry in Latvia?' Of course, my son sent me the money, and we gave half to one organization, and now the other half is for you."

Inguna was speechless. God had provided exactly what they needed. He wasn't going to stop. This was God's school, and he would meet the needs. Inguna embraced the old woman, and she left. More hard times would come, but Inguna knew God would provide at every turn; she wouldn't doubt again.

* * *

Lest we assume the glorious provision of God is limited only to those things we need, let me share a little more of Inguna's extraordinary life.

Two of my favorite stories from Inguna's journey didn't really fit in the earlier dialogue, but I knew I had to share them. As we consider what ministry looks like and how we might serve those around us with the beauty of salvation, love, and provision, let us not forget that sometimes just a toothbrush is enough to draw us to a deeper place with Jesus.

* * *

It was June 1993, a full four months before Inguna would travel to Texas to study, which she didn't even know was an option as she had not yet met John. Maris Dzelzs, who facilitated the discipleship training school, suggested that Inguna attend a two-week training in Finland (just north of Latvia across the Baltic). It would be the first foreign trip Inguna had ever taken. Her husband, Maris, was supportive of her going; and as an exhibition of his love for his sweet bride—remember that at this point he was not yet a believer—he pulled $250 from a drawer and shoved it into her hand so she'd have some spending money while she was gone. Inguna knew how significant and generous this was. Maris had spent the winter cutting trees and selling the lumber with a friend of his. Each man had made a profit of $250, and now he was giving his to his wife.

The training in Finland was extremely encouraging and emphasized the grave importance of being in the Word daily, but it wasn't the teaching Inguna recalled the most. Inguna was twenty-eight and still growing as a believer, but there were two older students there who invested in this young woman. Doubtless they had no idea how their kindness would affect her decades into the future. Harold was easily sixty, and one afternoon during a break in studies, the students went to buy some ice cream. Inguna knew she had the money Maris had given her, but she wanted to be careful not to spend it unnecessarily. Also, she had hopes of buying gifts for her family. As the students sat around enjoying their treats, Harold approached with an ice cream for Inguna. Her eyes welled with tears as she recounted that moment to me.

"I received millions in gifts later on, but that ice cream cone…" Her voice trailed off as she looked out the window in her office, and I could see her playing that moment on the screen of her mind. She blinked away the pictures and carried on with her story of that summer.

"I was twenty-eight, and this woman about fifty to fifty-five took me on a tour of the city during a break. We ended up at a toy store, and I remember praying in my mind, 'God, it is so difficult not to think of material things after all the things I've seen.' I found a toy oven for the girls, a suit for Maris, and a dress for myself. I wanted those things so badly, but I knew I didn't have very much money, and I was still trying not to spend what Maris had given me." Inguna thanked the woman for the tour, but even as she lay to sleep that night could not get those few items out of her mind. She so wanted to be able to surprise her family.

The two weeks quickly came to a close, and their last days were upon them. Inguna hadn't forgotten the things she had seen in town. Harold approached her, and she smiled warmly. He had become such a dear friend.

"Inguna, I need to talk to you," he said. "I want to give you some money to be able to buy gifts for your family." Inguna was stunned as Harold put more than a thousand Finnish crowns in her hand. It worked out to exactly $250. She bought the oven, the suit, the dress, a coffeemaker and a pair of shorts.

When she returned home with her packages, she could tell her husband was eyeing them all, counting and doing the math. She could see it on his face; he knew all the money was gone. It was then that she returned the same $250 he had given her before she left two weeks earlier.

Inguna had been challenged those two weeks, had grown, had been loved, and had come to see how God cared even about the little things. For surely, $250 and an ice-cream cone are a pittance compared to the cattle on a thousand hills.

The other story I loved begins even before Elina became sick. Maris and Inguna had seen pictures in a magazine of

Disney World, and Maris had promised her, "One day I will take you to Disney world."

* * *

Inguna breaks from the story to look at me and laugh, "He might as well have said, 'One day I'll take you to the moon.'" It just didn't seem like anything that could ever happen.

* * *

But we fast-forward to Valentine's Day 1994. Maris and Inguna were in Texas with their two children and another on the way. Maris had become a Christian since, and Inguna was working hard on her studies. Inguna had been invited to share her testimony at a Valentine's conference at a local church. She thought nothing of it, but two weeks later, she was called into the office at the school to take a phone call.

"Hello, you don't remember me, but my name is Wendell, and your testimony at the banquet really spoke to me so powerfully. My wife and I had our youngest die from a brain tumor. We moved from Florida to Texas, but when I was in Florida, I worked as a clown at Disney World. Anyway, I made some phone calls to my old boss and was able to get four free tickets for your family to go to Disney World."

Inguna couldn't believe it. She was so excited to be able to share the news with Maris and the girls. Of course, there was still the matter of getting to Florida, getting a place to stay, and paying for food.

The Sunday school class came through again, and though this wasn't food or necessary medical attention, the class all agreed that this family should be able to have a memorable vacation and raised eight hundred dollars to help send them to Florida. The car they had been driving wasn't likely to make the trip, but Maris insisted it would be fine. However, on the morning they were to leave, as they were headed to Joann's house to say good-bye, the car came to a sputtering halt. Joann rented them a car, and Wendell provided them a cooler full of food while Roy supplied them a credit card to get all their gas. The family was off.

The trip was a long one, and Maris enjoyed racing the cars on the interstate late at night. They stayed in the Motel 6, which according to Inguna was at the time "like the Hilton." They woke the next morning to go to the happiest place on earth. Elina had only one request—that Minnie would give her a kiss. Sure enough, as they were making their way along, Minnie Mouse came around the corner, and what else could she do but give this little girl a kiss and make her day?

Isn't it great how the little things can have such an overwhelming influence?

God Sustains the Preacher: Paul's Story

That God in his great grace provided for Paul is not even a question. From the moment he was converted, the Christian brethren cared for Paul.

Nothing had changed from yesterday to today. In this moment, Paul was clinging to the wreckage of the ship. Months ago, he had left for Rome as a prisoner, fully intending to appeal his case before Caesar. The last two weeks, neither the prisoners nor crew had eaten a bite, and the sun had remained concealed behind the thick wrappings of a storm. Just a day ago, the ship had struck a reef and had been beaten to pieces by the waves. Now every man was either swimming or clinging, like Paul, to the debris and slowly finding his way to shore. Voices could just scarcely be heard above the whistling of the wind and the breakers crashing on the rocks. Grown men had been reduced to howls and sobs like children. Paul, however, couldn't have felt more secure. It wasn't the first time he had been shipwrecked. It wasn't the first time he had to rely on the rescue that certainly would come from God the Creator and Sustainer. In Asia, he had previously been so deeply persecuted that he despaired of life itself. Even that had been used to strengthen his reliance on the God who raises the dead. Now, as he made his way through the blackness of night and the sea foam sought to choke him, thoughts of God's graciousness warmed his mind and body.

Years ago, he and Silas had been harshly beaten and chained, naked in a prison. But that didn't cause him to waver, and God had shown himself faithful even in that night, for as he and Silas raised their voices in song, an earthquake shook loose the doors, and the chains that bound them fell harmlessly to the ground. Paul smiled as he remembered the jailer and his family coming to salvation that night.

In Lystra, those who opposed the gospel had gathered round Paul and stoned him, dragging him from the city and leaving him for dead. But the disciples had gathered around him, and after praying for him, he stood back up whole and strong and returned to his work.

He had been rescued from Damascus by a basket. He had been welcomed by the believers in Jerusalem when Barnabas had made kind introductions. Then, of course, there was the church in Macedonia. They had perhaps been more helpful to him than any of the other churches to which he had ministered. Even when all other churches had withdrawn or withheld their loving provision, Macedonia had sought to fill every need of the road-weary apostle. He thought back to how this poverty-stricken body of believers had begged to share in the ministry of the saints in Jerusalem. He couldn't keep the smile from breaking across his face. They had supported all of his work in Thessalonica and even while he was preaching for eighteen months in Corinth. Paul fluttered with excitement as he remembered Epaphroditus, who had been the delivery agent of many of those gifts. What a fragrant offering those gifts had been.

Paul wasn't lazy. He refused to always seek the handout, though he would have been within his right to demand it. He had acquired the skill of tent making and had worked well at the job next to his dear friends Priscilla and Aquila. Those were fine days. They would preach in the synagogue or perhaps gather near the fire in a home and unfold, for all who had gathered round, the gospel message of Jesus. Then, as the day would draw to a close, Aquila would take his wife, Priscilla, by the hand, and they'd walk with Paul down the darkened streets of Corinth to a quiet place where they could work on the tents and talk of God and the Christ he had sent. In making and patching tents, Paul could be sure his needs were supplied well enough. When money was scarce, a gift would arrive in a timely fashion from Macedonia, and Paul would delight in the company of those who had been brought in and rejoice as they told of the work God was doing in Philippi and the surrounding regions.

Paul was never one to feel as though he lacked. There had been days of nakedness and days of hunger, but there had been more days of warm clothes and sated bellies. He was fully content in whatever circumstance he might face knowing there was nothing beyond his ability and considering it was Christ who would strengthen him for the task.

These memories and many more flooded his tired brain as he paddled with the waves. Just then, lightning split the sky, and the outline of an island revealed itself. Another flash, and the silhouettes of men could be seen running to and fro. Within moments, Paul brought his aging body to the sand and stood to his feet. The villagers there on Malta were kind to the castaways and helped to make a fire. The crewmen conducted a count to see who had made it safely to this island refuge, and Paul smiled a knowing smile, certain that God had saved every soul as he had declared he would. The fire sputtered and popped, bathing the wet men in an orange glow, and Paul grabbed a bundle of sticks to add to the blaze. No sooner had he done so than a viper struck and fastened itself onto Paul's hand. He shook it off into the flame as though it had been a fly or a speck of dirt and went about his business. Those around him expected he would soon swell up and die, but where men see death,

God can create life. God had purposed to take Paul to Rome to bear witness of Jesus there, and not a shipwreck or a viper would put a stop to that.

God had provided for him once again, and he slept the sleep of a man who knows no fear.

God Graciously Supplies:
Our Story

When we think of God's provisions in our life, we often think of those things we deem miraculous or wildly extraordinary. I've been doing ministry since the fall of 1997, and in the years that have passed, I have seen God provide for me so many times that I've lost count. I once considered journaling all the stories so one day I could put them all in a book, but many of them have since slipped my mind.

I was ten years old, and we attended Wilshire Park Baptist in Midland, Texas. Chris Osborne was the pastor back then. It must have been a Sunday night, and he was preaching on faith. I loved listening to him preach— or more accurately, I loved to watch him preach. He took up the entire stage. We were still fairly new to the church, and the previous pastor I knew stood anchored behind the pulpit. I just assumed that was the rule. Not Pastor Chris. He roamed everywhere. This particular night, he was preaching on faith, not unto salvation, but the kind of faith that trusted God with everything in life. I began to weep. Seriously, it would have been embarrassing if I hadn't been so struck to my heart. I jumped up and ran from the sanctuary and into the bathroom, colliding with a man who was just walking out.

"Are you okay, kid?" he asked.

I couldn't bring myself to look at him. I was so ashamed, but I sobbed, "I just realized I don't have any faith in God." I had been a Christian for several years already, but the idea of trusting God in my day-to-day life was foreign to me. That night as I went to bed, I prayed God would bring me to a place I could trust him for everything I ever needed.

About two years later—along with two different moves and different churches—I happened to overhear my mom and dad talking about how my father needed a raise. I hadn't forgotten my prayer for greater faith and felt this was a key moment. I took a piece of notebook paper from my desk and scrawled, "My dad will have a raise in three weeks," and then I added the date. I taped the piece of paper to the bookshelf on my desk and looked at it every day. Even at night, I could see the paper dance and bend under the influence of my ceiling fan, and seeing it would cause me to pray. One week passed, and then two. The days were coming to an end. Maybe I had been wrong. Maybe I should have put four weeks. But I kept praying. The day before the deadline was up, my dad came home and announced his raise. Now you should know that my dad is an excellent employee, and he has dominated every job he has ever had.

He was probably due the raise. He may have even requested it, but in the moment, I was rejoicing because God was taking care of my family. It strengthened my faith, and I knew God was going to provide for me.

When I was seventeen, I began the college application process. It was my senior year. Most people were filling out applications for any available five-hundred-dollar scholarship. I only filled out one. I wanted the biggest scholarship obtainable at that time. It was the one I needed, so it would be the one I would get. I didn't question it for a moment. Two months later, several names were called over the PA system, mine included, and we were asked to come to the office. As we all met in the corridor leading to the principal, people were wondering, "What's going on? What could this be about?" I smiled and replied, "We got the scholarship." Sure enough, they told us the news I already knew. God had provided a way for me to go to college (that I would later squander, but that is another story).

At thirty-one, I finally met the woman I was going to marry. Between the two of us, we had fifty-five thousand dollars in debt. Eleven thousand of that was credit card debt. We prayed diligently that God would erase the debt before we got married so we could be in a position to better honor him with our finances. Just weeks before we were married, we received a wedding gift of exactly eleven thousand dollars. The rest of the debt was paid off in our second year of marriage.

These are just some of the things I've experienced. I wish there was time to tell you of the groceries, the cars, the grape soda, the passports, and the toothbrush. Sometimes God gave me the ten dollars I needed, and sometimes he gave me the thousand dollars. There were times my food was scarce and my clothes were old. For years, I drove in the Texas heat without air conditioning. I've lived in rented rooms, trailers, ratty apartments, and small houses. I've had to crawl through my window to get in and out of my car, and I've had the same suit for thirteen years now. I've had medical bills we paid out for years, and I've had some paid anonymously. Sometimes we can pay all the bills at one time, and sometimes we have to spread them out through the month. Sometimes my family can go out to eat, and sometimes we run out of milk and bread three days before the next paycheck. But I still remain. I wake up every morning to face another day.

Do you still remain? You've had plenty, and you've had little, but you are still here, right? You've turned the leftovers into a casserole, and you've eaten the expensive cut of meat, haven't you (even if someone else bought it for you)? You know what it is like to get the bills paid just at the last moment and what it is like to be ahead. We have a lot of fat built into our system of needs these days. We could cut the cable if we had to, and the wireless Internet isn't a necessity. Unintelligent flip phones or prepaid plans could easily save us hundreds of dollars a year, and if we were just a little more disciplined, we could knock couponing out of the park. We haven't quite kept up with the Joneses, but we have what we need. How has it failed to occur to us that God is the one who has sustained us to this point? The spinach salad and bacon sandwich I had last night are just as much the provision of God as is the massive check or the plastic bag full of money for a Latvian school.

Our inability to see that God has sustained us dishonors him and his work. That we think less of the apple than we do of the car that finally has air conditioning is a commentary on the sad state of our theology. I've needed five dollars, and I've needed five thousand dollars. The stories we typically pass on are the ones we think will impress, but if we are desperate for five dollars and we have that need met, isn't it just as amazing and awe-inspiring as having the so-called grander need met? Need is need, right?

Okay, I have to tell you about the toothbrush. I was twenty-six and living with my friend Jed and his wife, Stacy. They let me live with them for three weeks while I was between homes. I was getting ready to move to a new city and was just really getting the full-time ministry going.

I had little money. I went to my local mega store and picked up deodorant, shampoo, bread—just the essentials. I spent everything but about thirty cents. On my way back to their house, I panicked. I had meant to buy a new toothbrush. Mine was more than a year old, and the bristles were falling out. I couldn't even afford a toothbrush. The thought struck me like a sledge hammer in the stomach. What made me think I could make it in ministry if I couldn't even shell out ninety-seven cents for my personal dental hygiene? You know how that feels, right? It isn't the huge thing that cripples you. It is when we can't even do the little thing that we are shaken to our core. A thousand doubts and fears flooded my brain, and my heart raced. But when I got back to my friend's house, there on the counter in the guest bathroom was a brand-new toothbrush with a note: "I noticed you needed a new toothbrush, so I bought this for you today. — Stacy." Like I said, a need is a need. You have toothbrush stories of your own. In fact, in just a moment, when you put this book down to get dinner started or go to buy the kids new shoes for soccer, I want you to stop and think about how you have the food and the money for the shoes because God has sustained you to this point.

I'll go to bed tonight, and my air conditioning may go out, but I'll be sustained. Our grocery budget is already strained for the month, but we'll get by. I have no preaching engagements for the duration of the year and will run out of money with three months still to come, but I've been here before, and God will not forget us.

As long as we are sustained, we can say God still moves among us. And even should we suffer or die in our faithful pursuit of God, we can be confident that he has sustained us to the very day he had planned for us before the ages began.

The Ministry:
Inguna's Story

I was exhausted. A full day and a half earlier, I had met Ken in Dallas, and we flew the red eye to London. We filled our bellies with fish and chips and then caught a flight to Helsinki, Finland. We missed the last flight to Riga, Latvia, and it was late. The hotel restaurant was serving dinner for a few more minutes, so we grabbed something to eat. I tried the reindeer meat. We were up at five in the morning to catch our final flight. The airport in Riga wasn't busy, and we were the only ones in line for the rental car. We still had nearly two hours by car to Talsi. My brain was trying hard to prepare. What were the questions I needed to ask? I'm only here for three days. What do I need to see? I'm supposed to write an entire book on something about which I know nothing. What if I do a bad job?

Ken is a great companion for a weary brain and overall just a good guy to travel with. He knows a little bit about everything and carries the conversation well amid my tired grunts and nods. Somehow he is still laughing and smiling. His heavy white and gray facial hair dances as he speaks. He is in love with Latvia, which explains how he seems to be more and more energized with every kilometer we travel. For me, Latvia is still a stranger. We've just done the polite introductions, but I'm hoping we will become friends.

"This is Talsi," he says, his words dusting away some of the cobwebs.

Now it is time to work. We pass a couple of cemeteries on our way into town. The road winds to the left with a lake down the hill on the right. Just beyond the lake, a white steeple pierces the cloudy sky. The streets are narrow; some are cobblestone, which gives the city a classic faraway feel. The buildings are distinctly European—with the exception of the plain remnants of the Soviet era buildings—and strike me as familiar. The place feels quaint, though I don't know that I've ever used that word to describe anything before. If you were telling fairytales, Talsi would be the city that emerges from the fog in the opening pages.

"I could live here." The words come from my mouth and surprise me a little, but the place itself feels very homey. There is Martinelli's, a nice restaurant just around from the school. We'd eat every meal there for three days, and should you ever visit, you won't want to miss the fresh pork chops slathered with mushrooms and served with potatoes and salad. Don't forget to save room for the apple crisp. You'll have to wait; there is one cook. The white stucco walls on the outside, with the deep set windows, seem inviting. But the flower boxes are empty for now. It is still too cold. The lights break out into the shadows of the evening, advertising that there is room at one of the eight tables inside. If you walk down the hill a little more, you'll be right by the lake. Head up the hill, and there is the old Lutheran church. As you walk back from Martinelli's, you pass the grocery store. It is small, but it has everything one needs. Fresh bread is ready to pick up, so we grab some with butter and jam. This will make a nice snack for later when the town goes to sleep. Ken buys the same kind of milk and cookies he discovered years ago on his first visit.

We pull up next to the school and park by Inguna's car. We walk up the steps into the office. To our right, a secretary greets us. There is a table with freshly made banana bread sliced and ready to be eaten. I take a piece, because you just don't pass on banana bread. Inguna's office is immediately to our left, the door facing the secretary's desk. We poke our heads in, and Inguna smiles.

"Well, well, I see you made it," she says. "Okay, I have a few things to do. We will get your key to the room and then we will begin. Are you hungry? We can eat lunch. Maris will join us tonight for supper."

Inguna and Ken are a lot alike in the way they both have scores of thoughts and usually fire them off one right after the other. Inguna grabs a key and walks us into a hallway.

We turn left and then immediately take the door on our right. It is a chemistry lab about the size of a large walk-in closet or a small dining room. Thousands of tiny glass bottles and beakers line metal shelves, and there is a distinct smell of chemicals in the air that reminds me of high school. A model skeleton hangs out in the corner, and on the counter is an anatomically correct torso with removable organs; that guy would startle me every time I came down the stairs for the next three days.

Inguna uses the key to unlock the door at the back of the lab, and we head up narrow, shifting stairs on which apparently more than one visiting missionary has twisted an ankle. I make my way deliberately and carefully to the top as the stairs turn up and to the left at a small landing. I find myself in another hallway. This one has three or four guest rooms, each outfitted with several beds and a desk. Ken grabbed the one on the right—I got the feeling it was his—and I duck into one across the hall. Two bathrooms with showers and a laundry bookend the hallway. A small kitchen with a table sits at the far end of the hall with a couple of couches just to the side. When people come to work with Talsi Christian School, this is where they stay. We unpack and a few minutes later head back down the stairs and through the chemistry lab; I flinch at the model torso on the counter.

Across from the door that leads up the stairs is one that is open into a classroom. Several students turn and glance at us before they go back to the lecture. Back into the hallway we go, past the office, down a little slope where the old building meets the new. Elina is sitting at her desk in the hallway preparing to ring the bell to signal the end of class, and she lights up when she sees us. She was expecting us, and she can't wait to give me the tour. We are feeling peckish, so she leads us down a hallway to the right and into the dining hall. On the wall are many colored signs with the names of those who have given to the school or worked there. I recognize one or two. The kitchen staff is still there, cleaning up from the morning and making final preparations for the lunch rush. Glasses, silverware, and plates have already been set on all the tables along with baskets of bread. Pickle soup is for lunch, and we are offered a bowl. We sit down with our apple juice and soup and just take a moment to catch our breath. Ken dives into his food, but I'm still taking in everything. At the end of the rather large dining area are some room dividers with children's artwork tacked to them. One of the tables is reserved for the teachers. Elina buzzes with excitement. Lunch is over, and we head back to Elina's desk. If we turn left, we will be going back to the office; to the right we enter a narrow hall. Lockers are on the left a few steps more, and to the right is the beautiful new gym. Some students are bustling back and forth, paying no mind to their spectators. Elina leads me upstairs, and we visit every classroom along the way.

The school is very nice. On the outside is the striking red roof that covers each building and the large stones set into the walls. The older buildings have small circular windows near the point of the roof and large deep-set windows framed by red brick. A brick circular drive sits next to the backside of the building. There is a field just out my window where I watch some of the younger children run and play in the cool April weather. God built this ministry, and he isn't done with it yet. It staggers me that I was invited in to be a part of this work. I say a quick prayer asking God to help me be a blessing as I seek to capture the heart of this wonderful, beautiful place. Maybe I'm not the guy for the job; the thought stabs at me. These people need someone who can truly help them, who can bring real attention to their ministry. That thought stabs more deeply. I swallow hard. God brought me here. I can trace my presence here back to one guy from eight years earlier. God brought me here. I just need to be faithful. I will. I will be faithful with this ministry, and I will tell their story.

Talsi Christian School draws students from Christian and non-Christian families alike. The opportunity for a student to receive a good education has been the enticing force for most of the area families. But Talsi Christian School has higher ambitions than just a formal education. Inguna and each of her staff are deeply concerned with the spiritual life of each student. One of the teachers said in an interview, "The most special and precious moments are when a student says, 'I believe in God.'"

The school is at an enrollment of 250 children now—up from thirty-seven in its first year. It started as just an elementary school that fall day in 1995, but by 1998, it had to expand to accommodate children through ninth grade. In 2005, it required another building project to make enough room for tenth through twelfth grade, add a gym, and make things handicap-accessible. A single check of five hundred thousand dollars from a woman named Lou paid for the gym. Inguna received it as a personal check and was once again staggered at the provision of God. Talsi Christian has won an award as the best urban high school in Latvia several times since 2005. Now the school is out of room again, and with the government help all but gone, the possibility of expansion and even keeping the teachers paid has become tenuous at best.

There were two particular student testimonies that stuck out to me while I was there. One young woman named Jana shared a story of how she really wanted to come to TCS for high school, but there was just no money for it.

She began to pray that God would provide the 200 Lats needed for tuition. After she finished her junior high years, she received a card and a financial gift. It was exactly the money she needed to the last cent! More telling than that, however, is that in December 2012, her mother suddenly died in a car accident. It was the love her teachers and fellow classmates showed her that solidified for her that TCS was the place she was supposed to be.

* * *

"They just cried with me," Jana recalled. "It was then I was 100 percent sure God wants me to be here. I want to be where God wants me to be."

* * *

A male student named Toms joined Ken and me for lunch one afternoon when classes let out. We drove downtown for a slice of pizza. Yes, you can get pizza in Talsi—and you won't be disappointed. Toms really wants to be a preacher when he finishes school, but his parents aren't convinced yet. Most Latvian parents want to see their children get an education in a field that could make them financially stable, and though preaching would be a fine hobby, it doesn't fit the bill for a life skill. Toms is decidedly in love with Jesus.

*   *   *

"I accepted Jesus in my heart, and from that moment on, nothing was the same. This huge strength of God came into me," he said. "This school is just different from all the others." He couldn't be more right.

*   *   *

After the inaugural year of classes, TCS hosted its first orphan camp. There was a baby boy, eight months old and abandoned, who has grown up in the TCS summer camp system. He is now nearly nineteen, a believer, and is pursuing carpentry school. Inguna has forgotten very little of the children she has poured into for so long. The orphan camp continues every summer. Inguna remembers just pulling up to the orphanage and loading the children into a bus. These children were part of her ministry, and she loved them deeply.

The orphan camp isn't the only camp Talsi Christian School operates. Every summer, it hosts discipleship camp, sports camp, youth camp, and teacher's camp. Inguna is committed to leaving a lasting legacy of Christ in her home country.

"Most kids have never heard of Christ," she said. "Many became believers and honor God in their workplaces and universities now. We've even had former students serve as missionaries in Albania, South Africa, Indonesia, and Canada."

That morning, so many years ago now, that Elina woke up paralyzed was no surprise to God. We were fortunate enough while there to celebrate Elina's birthday along with the staff of the school. She took a seat, and one by one, students and teachers lined up to give her flowers and gifts. The presents piled up around her feet as different individuals stopped to say a few words. Several music students played a song for the birthday girl, and finally, everyone posed for pictures. Elina is vibrant and happy, completely in love with Jesus and all those around her. You can't help but be in awe of how God used the life of this young woman to bring people from all over the world into a saving relationship with Jesus. It was part of the story—part of his story for a Latvian family.

The story included a dusty Lutheran church and a faithful old pastor. There was a hasty prayer made to an unknown God. The fall of the iron curtain, the arrival of missionaries, a phone number on a piece of paper, a training program, the gospel, a garden, a purpose—they all led to this day. The story isn't finished. Not one of us who has walked the halls of the school or had tea at Inguna's desk believes the story is finished. It's just time to turn the page. It's time to find new people to include in the work being done. For us, tomorrow remains unwritten, but our good and gracious God has carried his work to this point. Thousands of children have come to know the Lord, and those children have become adults who are traveling the world to make Christ known. Inguna now spends her time watching and participating in the movement of God as the gospel is proclaimed, love is lavished, and provision is extended to each needful person in and around Talsi.

Inguna says it best: "With God, usually things start out small. It's one person, one individual, who is willing to do more than just live his average life."

The Sowing of the Gospel: Paul's Story

Paul knew it was going to be difficult for him to do the ministry of the gospel among the Jews. They all knew him too well. They knew of his former way of life as a Pharisee and as a persecutor of the church. That didn't mean Paul didn't have a place to work. His friend Barnabas came to Tarsus looking for him. Barnabas had been spending time in Antioch, and they were really in need of discipleship. God's grace had fallen on the city, and it was growing rapidly. It didn't take much to convince Paul to return to Antioch with Barnabas, and they spent an entire year there teaching a great many people.

Paul didn't stop his work at Antioch. In time, the church there sent both Paul and Barnabas on their first mission. City after city and synagogue after synagogue, the two men proclaimed the word of God. Across sea and land they traveled, reading from the Scripture faithfully.

Paul tenaciously taught the gospel over three separate trips in numerous cities and saw thousands come to know Jesus as Savior. Those who opposed him beat him and left him for dead, flogged him, arrested him, mocked him, and hounded him from town to town. Paul never quit. He ministered in the homes of the saintly few and addressed the masses from the center of the city. He preached into the midnight hours to those who had come to consider him family and exhorted the pagans to turn to Jesus while in the market places.

His ministry didn't take one particular shape or form, and he certainly wasn't limited to a single location, but the thrust of his ministry was Jesus Christ and Christ crucified. Wherever Paul went, and whatever he did, he made certain he would know nothing more and boast in nothing other than the cross (1 Cor. 2:2; Gal. 6:14).

Taking Up the Mantle: Our Story

There is an imagined gap between the front row of chairs in the church and the pastor on the stage. I don't mean the obvious gap of carpet. I mean many times, the people in the chairs look at the guy on the stage and think he is somehow godlier than they are. Every lunch I've ever been to, every sort of event, people turn to me and say, "Pastor, would you mind praying?" Certainly I don't mind praying, but my prayers aren't more valid because I'm a preacher. I'm not better than the people sitting in the seats on Sunday. I am righteous because of the blood of Christ just like Abraham, just like you, just like anyone who has called upon the name of Jesus. I have a direct line to God not because I'm clergy but because Jesus is my intercessor. The insecure laypeople are often convinced that ministry is for the church staff alone. They bring us their neighbors and coworkers in the hope we would do our pastoral thing and get them saved. Ministry is left to those who are paid to do it full time. Of course, this is just a misunderstanding of who we are in Christ.

Sure, the theoretical gap goes both ways. Many pastors think they are better than their church members. Many of us rest on our laurels and convince ourselves of our superiority. We boast and brag in how many people we have at the church or how many people we've led to the Lord as though the beauty of the gospel has something to do with us. We sometimes snort in derision that a layperson would question our teaching or dare to disagree. We occasionally persuade ourselves that the work of God must be carried out according to our agenda, our purposes, and our ideas—or not at all. We micromanage every single area of every ministry in our church, believing we are somehow the CEO or the president elect and that it is our job to run the show. Of course, this is just sinful arrogance.

Certainly not every pastor in the pulpit is a raging egomaniac, and not every layperson feels inferior or small compared to those who teach and preach the Word. Yes, I am a preacher—not because I'm superior but because that is the gifting with which the Holy Spirit has entrusted me. I preach because I must, and I get paid because the Bible teaches that those who preach the gospel should earn their living from the gospel. But that in no way means that I alone, or pastors in general, should be the only ones doing ministry. Each of us as believers should be about the business of bringing the gospel to the world and living it out in our personal lives.

Like Paul, we need to come to the place where we know nothing more than Jesus and him crucified, where we boast in nothing but the cross. It matters little what our daily job is or how we spend our time from hour to hour if the focus of those days and hours is centered on knowing Christ and making him known.

I have a dear friend who is a passionate preacher. He used to travel all the time and do various events around the country, but now he primarily stays home. He is the chaplain for the local college football team. He coaches gymnastics. He is a personal trainer. He works with young men on their physical and spiritual fitness. He doesn't take the church stage as often as he used to, but he is no less a minister.

Another man is a pilot for a national airline. He lives in Houston with his wife and children. He faithfully teaches a senior Sunday school class and opens the doors to his house on a weekly basis for food and additional Bible study.

A woman I know, an empty nester, scarcely has a week go by that she hasn't had women over for lunch and welcomed them into her home. She and her husband, who works for a bank, constantly disciple young couples who are preparing for marriage.

A friend of mine in East Texas has preached in one capacity or another for more than twenty years. In the last few years, his life has turned to a job in the medial sales industry, yet he still teaches, disciples, and trains families on his left and right hand.

I recently met a young man, seventeen years old, who was passionately in love with Jesus. He said he really wanted to be a surfer, but to better honor God, he thought perhaps he should grow up to be a pastor. I laughed. He already looked the part of surfer—shell necklace, blond hair to his jaw and board shorts—all he lacked was an ocean. I asked him, "Do you think surfers need to know about Jesus?" The answer was obvious, and he nodded his head. I'm pale, dark-haired, uncoordinated, and far from athletic, so I inquired who between the two of us is more likely to fit in with the surfer crowd on the beach. He and the other students with him laughed. Again, the answer was obvious. So I told him to grow up and move to Florida, California or Hawaii and be a surfer who passionately loves Jesus, to learn to make surfboards and become the best at it. Then, when fully immersed in that world, just keep loving Jesus and teaching others to do the same. His smile spread clear across his face, as he said, "You mean I could really do that?" I nodded with the reply, "Just love Jesus while you are doing it."

My sons are currently five and four. One wants to be an animal photographer and explorer while the other wants to study penguins. I constantly remind them they can do whatever they want so long as they love Jesus while doing it. We have got to quit thinking of ministry as something the pastor does. Ministry is and always has been the proclamation of the cross of Christ. We would do good to realize that our opportunity for ministry doesn't have to be waiting for us on the annual church mission trip or when we finally get a seminary education. Are you a hairstylist? Then you have a place to proclaim the cross. Do you sell cars? Then you have an opportunity to give your coworkers Jesus. Are you a doctor? You have a greater peace to offer the hurting family members than they have ever known. Are you a teacher? There are children under your charge who do not know any kind of love at home, and you can show them the love of Christ. Are you a mother with a handicapped child? Perhaps you should start a Christian school.

The Church:
Christ's Beautiful Body

The body of Christ should be concerned with no other thing than bringing salvation to the nations, loving each other and the world as Christ does, and seeking to meet the needs of those who are lacking. If the church would do these things with diligence, then we would find there is more than enough room for each of us to minister faithfully. In Acts 9, we learn of a woman named Tabitha who had a gracious ministry of caring for the widows in her community. She was a prolific seamstress and made all manners of garments for these dear old ladies. When she died suddenly, it struck to the heart of the widows, and they implored Peter to do something. Graciously, God allowed Peter to raise Tabitha back to life. Her ministry to these saints was not done yet.

Lydia was a shop owner. She dealt in fine fabrics. Upon coming to know the truth of Jesus, she opened her house to Paul and Silas when they were in the area. Even after Paul and Silas had been beaten, imprisoned, and then later released, she gave the men sanctuary (Acts 16).

There was no needy person among the believers in Jerusalem because no one considered any possessions as belonging to oneself alone. Rather everyone shared all things in common. Barnabas sold a field he owned to supply the needs of the saints gathered in Jerusalem (Acts 4). Simon the tanner opened up his home to Peter on his travels in Acts 10. As we have already seen, the church in Macedonia sought to be a blessing to the saints in Jerusalem, and the Philippian church specifically met the needs of Paul as he was traveling and preaching.

We see then even in these few but significant examples that ministry isn't limited to the preacher. In fact, the whole of the body of Christ, you and I included, should be about the work of making Jesus known. Furthermore, as believers we have been endowed by the Spirit of God with spiritual gifts for the building up of the body of Christ. Only a few of the gifts are what we might call the preaching gifts: evangelism, preaching/teaching, apostleship, and prophecy. Only a few of the remaining gifts are what we might call unique: speaking in or interpretation of tongues, healing, utterances of wisdom or knowledge. But the remainder of the gifts we typically—and sinfully—consider mundane: faith, spiritual discernment, help/service, administration, encouragement, giving, leadership, and mercy (1 Cor. 12; Rom. 12; Eph. 4; 1 Pet. 4).

But there is no one gift that outshines the others. I am an insecure preacher who would fail at this work without those around me who have encouraged me and financially contributed to the work. I need someone on my side who can bring administration to my sloppy and disorganized world. But the encourager and the giver and the administrator need me as well. Not one of us is sufficient unto ourselves. Lest these gifts are joined together as the hand is joined to the wrist and the head to the neck and shoulders, we will not be doing the ministry of the church. This ministry we are called to as a church isn't an individual race; it is not a solo effort. We are united together in and through Christ for the express purpose of making Christ known and boasting in his cross through which salvation and sanctification have been given.

What Remains for Us to Do?

First and foremost, I hope you are encouraged. I hope you have begun to recognize that the things regularly dismissed as common are actually the greatest works of God. There is no higher work of God than the cross of Christ. Furthermore, you have been adopted into a family that will love you and care for you while doing life next to you. Not only so, but you have also been sustained by God to this point in your life. It hasn't always been easy, and certainly there have been wearisome days, but even now you can recognize that you trust God more deeply and know him more personally than you did previously. If this were not enough, God has also equipped you with gifts to benefit and bless the body of Christ and has filled you with the power of the Spirit that is necessary for using those gifts effectively. These gifts are supernatural in their nature and are evidence that God is powerfully at work in your heart. Sure, you may or may not one day see a blind man recover his sight, a dead girl raised to life, or bread multiplied for the masses; but all those things pale in comparison to the beauty of the cross, the church, and the work of the Spirit through you.

The kingdom of heaven now stands at the threshold of time, waiting to break through the clouds with triumphant glory as Jesus, your Lord, descends. The trump will sound, and the voice of the archangel will resound and shake the foundations of the mountains. The whole of the world will bow before him whose white robe drips with blood. His eyes will burn like torches of fire, and a double-edged sword will come from his mouth. Upon his thigh will be written "King of kings and Lord of lords." Not a single tongue in the crowd will ask in a mocking tone, "What work have you ever done among us?" for in that moment, every soul will know how God has moved. Every eye will be opened to the magnitude of the severity and blessing that sprung forth from the veins of Jesus at Calvary. Every heart will recognize the beautiful unity of Christ's bride, the church, made whole and spotless without any hint of sin or shame. No mind will doubt the gracious provision of God as it reflects on the temporary days it walked the earth.

So be blessed. Feel rich. God is no less today than he has ever been. It is true that you are made more into his likeness with each passing day as the Spirit causes you to be conformed to the pattern of your glorious Savior. Sin is daily being overthrown in your heart. Love swells like a tsunami and pours forth where it had not before. God's power charges through you and rouses you from sleep with vitality to live and work the gifts and ministry he has written on your heart. Beloved, he is here.

Secondly, I hope you will find a way to serve. Just by purchasing this book, you have already made a donation to Talsi Christian School, but don't let it end there. Someone in your church, your community, is seeking to serve the Lord. Come alongside him and pray with him. Buy him an ice cream. Take him to lunch. Serve your brother or sister in Christ. Disciple and pour the Scripture over that person a thousand times. You and I may never be the people who leave our little towns; I sit here in the back of a borrowed office at a local church. The sky is heavy with clouds, and a gentle rain is falling on this warm September day. The rain is needed here in West Texas. As I look out the window, I know this is home for me. About 85 percent of the people in this town don't know Jesus. This is where I need to be. Inguna still lives in Talsi, the city in which she was raised. Nearly half a century later, she still calls it home. You and I don't have to travel the world to serve God. Someone has to stay home. If everyone always left, there would have been no Sunday school class to pour into Inguna's family. If everyone always left, who would share Christ with those who live and work around us? Who shares Jesus with Daniel at the supermarket I use or Craig, the owner of the local pizza place, or Ashley, the girl who works the register at my favorite Mexican food restaurant?

You and I may not be the people who go, but if we stay, we must not be lazy. We stay for the work at hand. We stay to proclaim the powerful work of God. We stay to proclaim that there is a God in Heaven who sent his Son, Jesus, to die on the cross. We bear witness that this Jesus put an end to sin and to death and was raised back to life on the third day. We explain that this same Jesus will come back for us one day, and those who have put their faith in him will be saved to life everlasting. We don't leave the work to those who have gone; rather, we partner with them to ensure that the work is getting done here. We walk out our front doors, and we find people who need Jesus. And having found them in their need, we supply it.

We shower one another with love. We care for our fellow believers and pray for them. The world comes to know we are believers in Jesus by how we treat one another. We cease from our backbiting and gossip. We put aside all things that cause schisms and divisions among us, and we seek to be unified in faith and purpose. We look with grace on our weaker brethren, or if we are the weaker ones, we look with grace on those whose freedom in Christ we find unsettling. We hold each other accountable to Christ but not to our own personal standards. We quickly forgive those who have wounded us, choosing to forsake all records of wrong. We seek out ways to do good to the household of faith. Oh, how wonderful it will be when the fallen world sees us lifting up one another rather than striking with fists and tongues. The church will become evident, for there will be no denying her great familial love and concern. Then the bride will have moved closer to what she was always meant to be.

So we stay and share the greatest story ever. We love those who share the pew with us from week to week—and those who have warmed the pew down the street. But we also seek to be used by God to provide for those who lack. Where we have gathered much, we must be generous and gracious. We do not give such that we are burdened but so that there be no lack among us. We give our five dollars a month or five thousand to ensure that those who left us to carry out the work of God are equipped to do so. We make sure that the father training pastors in Guatemala has enough money to care for his family of five so they may persist in their work. We give to the young church-planting pastor in our community so his family can have groceries while he seeks to honor God in his preaching. We not only listen to the young nurse from Africa and her tales of salvations and baptisms in dirty rivers or puddles, but we make sure she has the medicine and the Bibles she needs so she can continue. We send resources to the elder couple in Spain who have given the last thirty years of their married life to reach the hardened hearts of those along the sea. And yes, we send money and people to Talsi Christian School so Inguna can continue to provide not just an education for the youth of Latvia but also that she may give them Jesus. We want her youth camps and orphan camps to continue. We have gathered much so those among us with little can be amply supplied.

God is working. He has saved us, loved us, and provided for us.

God is working.

Let us work too.

We were not saved that we might sit idly by and bide our time until the gates of heaven swing wide. God has moved magnificently among us, and so by his great power, we too shall move magnificently among the world.

A Portrait of Inguna

I think it is important you get a sense of Inguna, that you be able to picture her and know her heart. I have tried to describe her in vivid detail when the opportunity was afforded me in the story. As of the writing of this book, Inguna is forty-nine years old. She looks younger for sure. As I've said, she has dark black hair that hangs well past her shoulders. Her bangs rest casually on her eyebrows. Her eyes are bright, and I don't just mean their green-blue color. She is clearly happy. I am glad to have met her now and wonder at the sadness she must have carried in her eyes at the beginning of our story. Her smile is a broad one that stretches halfway across her face. Her cheekbones are high and prominent, made more so by her constant smile. There is the faintest dimple nestled just to the left of her mouth. Her fingernails are always painted brightly—today red, tomorrow probably purple. She dresses sharply and carries herself with confidence. She is never indifferent, and no one has to wonder what she is thinking. Perhaps it is the years of running a school, or perhaps it is just her personality, but she is decisive and prompt. Her laugh is almost as readily available as her tears, and each punctuates her storytelling with ease. She is hospitable but also quick to business. She won't waste anyone's time, and she would ask that no one waste hers. Some could describe her as curt, but I don't think I'd ever say such a thing. Perhaps it is that we in the States are too subtle and in many cases too cowardly to say what ought to be said—not so with Inguna. But I have always liked it when people are direct with me. I never once had to question what she was trying to say or question her motives.

She speaks of the Bible with ease, and it is clear that the woman who found it difficult to get into the Word the first few years of knowing Christ no longer finds it a challenge. Even when she talks of the school or the book or the needs she is facing, she does so with a matter-of-fact tone that doesn't sway to worry or fear. She knows what is needed, and she knows God, who has cared for her thus far. She sees how God has moved in her life from before her salvation, and it comforts her even now.

She loves her husband deeply. Having the opportunity to eat with them both and see them talk and laugh was refreshing. Maris himself is less boisterous than his wife but is a delight to know. Inguna adores all three of her children; Zane and Janis live in the States while Elina lives at home. Her mother is still one of her closest friends.

In the telling of this story, you will notice I have not told of any bad guys or villains, but each of us knows there must have been at least one. It is true that along the way there were people who had at one time or another helped Inguna who later turned on her and the school. There are players in this story who fell into great sin and abandoned all affections for God and their families. There are devastating hurts and grievous wounds that have not yet been mended, but Inguna, proving her character, has asked that I politely leave out these details. She recognizes even now those who are away from God were still used by him to bring her to this place. She would still have them restored to God and have their marriages made whole. She is quick to point out that telling the shameful things that have been wrought do nothing to bring honor and glory to God, nor does it help the work God is doing in Latvia, and I appreciate her all the more for her graciousness.

Inguna has been used mightily by God and will be for years to come. God will cause the school to flourish, or he will use her in some other—as of yet unknown—way. You can be sure that God will faithfully provide for Inguna, but you may want to prayerfully consider how you can serve the youth and families of Latvia. Ask God how your church, Bible study, women's group, men's group, youth group, or family could be a blessing to Inguna and Talsi Christian

School. God may be inviting you to partner with him in this work being done on the other side of the globe. You may be thinking you don't have enough surplus to make a difference, but even the ice-cream cone matters. You can send any sizes of gifts to the following:

Talsi Christian School fund (tax deductible)
4:13 Ministries
PO Box 202556
Arlington, TX 76006
USA

Talsi Christian School fund (tax deductible)
Lamar Baptist Church
Att Lynne Parra
1000 W Lamar Blvd.
Arlington, TX 76012
USA

Bible Study
for Further Understanding

I hope you have enjoyed these stories and that you feel encouraged by what God continues to do. For those of you who wish to go into more of the theology behind the primary work of God being centered on the cross, love, and provision, I invite you to take some time in the following pages. There are three in-depth studies corresponding to each of the topics discussed above. In the following pages I spend a little time helping to unfold for you the biblical underpinnings that beautifully give shape and weight to the stories I've told. I hope you will take the time to read these last pages and meditate on the Scripture and its glorious richness.

God's Greatest Movement: Salvation

I think when our salvation comes to light in our childhoods, it is often difficult to think of ourselves as having been changed all that much. We think in terms that are foreign to heaven and build righteousness based on our own standards. We think of ourselves as innocent children in need of saving but not so much as the rebellious fiends cursing on the corner. We understand we are sinners, but we tend to look down our noses at those we suppose are worse sinners, never understanding that we need a Savior just as much as those who wear rebellion like a badge of honor.

Perhaps that is why so many of us who grew up in the Bible belt of American culture find our stories uninspired. I've heard people say of the day God changed their lives, "My testimony isn't that great. I wasn't doing drugs or sleeping around or stealing things. I just grew up going to church, and one day at Vacation Bible School when I was about eight, I asked God to save me." People lament that they weren't saved away from human corruption into a life of holiness, and some even seem to pine for a better tale to tell. On the flip side, there are those who boast and brag in their wickedness and their wretchedness and then only lightly speak of God saving them from their pugnacious lifestyles. We seem to applaud those stories more than the ones of children converted on the laps of their dear grand-mothers while eating up freshly made cookies. We act as though the saving work of God is less impressive when there is less sinfulness to overcome.

Therein lies our problem. We have misunderstood the depth of our corruption and the greatness of the beautiful, powerful, merciful grace of God. We weren't saved from various degrees of sin; we were saved from its power. We were redeemed from damnation and not varying degrees of judgment. We were justified not for a moment but for all eternity as our Intercessor sits at the right hand of the Father. We were made into new creatures, holy and beloved, chosen and accepted— not just polished-up versions of our former sinful selves.

Our story is beautiful! When was the last time you talked about the greatest work of God in your life? I do not mean the healing, the money, the strength of emotive response, but the day he brought you from death to life. Remember the day your mind was quickened to fathom and embrace the wonderful grace of God Almighty? Think about that day! Share it again with your spouse. Tell your children again of the day God broke through your stony heart. Boast of the cross among your friends as you fill them with the hope of truly knowing Jesus. There is no greater movement of God in our lives than that we who did not know him have come to know him.

I want you to stop and reflect on what you have just read.

The greatest work of God in Inguna's life isn't found in the telling of her ministry. It is found in the truth of Jesus breaking through the veil of death and bringing a soul to life. The most profound thing about Paul isn't that he wrote two-thirds of the New Testament and planted dozens of churches; it is that he who hated Jesus was overthrown by love and into love. We wonder how God is moving in our lives, and certainly from this point forward, he will work in many and glorious ways. But they will all pale in comparison to the saving work he has done in the depths of our hearts through the cross of Jesus.

I have preached in many settings and at many events since 1997, and almost every one of them begins with gathering all the people together and praying in earnest that God would move. Now what has been meant by "move" depends on the group of people I had the opportunity of working with at any given moment.

The marriage conferences usually want to see marriages strengthened or restored.

The youth retreats desire to see young people living boldly for Jesus in their schools.

The revivals want to see renewed vigor in all things Jesus.

If the group is more charismatic in its leanings, then it seeks a physical manifestation of the Spirit.

If more conservative and buttoned up, the group tends to look for a deeper affection.

Sometimes the prayer for God's movement is really a thinly veiled request for a financial gift.

Sometimes the prayer seems to be a recitation borne out of years of monotony.

There isn't anything inherently wrong with praying for these things, but unfortunately, it indicates a lack of acknowledgement that the best movement of God is through his saving work in the lives of men and women. If we are really honest with ourselves, all of us at one point or another categorize the work of God by the things we see in terms of money, health, or emotions. We declare with excitement that God moved and the offering was just enough to meet the needs of the new building project. We rejoice as we boast in the fact God brought healing to the one for whom the doctors had no hope. We leave a particularly charged sermon and contemplate the movement of God in us as we feel fresh and joyful. We delight people with the signs and wonders we've seen God do, and we boast in the wisdom he has imparted to us. But truly, if we seek signs and wisdom as the indication God has moved, we have likely missed the point. In 1 Corinthians, Paul reminds the church, "Jews demand signs and Greeks seek wisdom…but to those who are called, both from the Jews and Greeks, Christ is the power of God and the wisdom of God" (1:22–24).

Think on that for a moment; Christ is both the power and the wisdom of God. There is no work God can do on this planet that will demonstrate more power than he did through the cross. There is no book or collection of books that could ever contain more wisdom than that which is found in the resurrected Jesus.

It is imperative that we understand this point, not only so our boasting will be planted firmly in Christ rather than the things we've seen and known but also that we might rightly think of God's work. Paul reminds the church that Christ is both the fullness of wisdom and power. You and I have both met the individuals who say if we could prove the presence of God, then they would believe. We might amuse them with tales of healings, angels, miraculous provision, and the secrets of the supernatural realms, but the truth of Jesus is better than these things. A person being healed of terminal cancer is not a greater testimony of God's power than Jesus being fully divine. Angels appearing before us and wielding words or swords is small in terms of power when compared to divine Jesus becoming man like us. The testimony of provision with regard to money and resources is earthly and frail when held up against the divine man on the cross who provides escapes from both sin and death for all men. Spiritual warfare and manifestations fall by the wayside when one remembers that Christ split sin's power asunder and with tremendous force overthrew the grave. It isn't that we can't speak of all tangible earthly things God has done for us or through us, but we must remember that our greatest boast will always be in the cross.

There is no power on earth or in heavenly places greater than the person of Jesus, for "by him all things were created, in heaven and on earth, visible and invisible, whether thrones or dominions or rulers or authorities—all things were created through him and for him" (Col. 1:16). People continue to demand signs and pray for the movement of God, but in truth, Jesus is the zenith of all signs and all movement. There is no thing higher than Jesus. There is not a single movement of God we could point to that carries more weight and glory than the movement of God through the great gospel news of Jesus Christ. When we pray for God to move and we have in mind even acceptable requests like provision and healings, we must recognize that the greatest movement of God for which we could implore him is the movement of Jesus.

He is also the epitome of wisdom, whereas all the books and learning we could ever amass in our stay on this earth would be like taking in a thimbleful of ocean and saying we have mastered its depths. God mocks the sum total of earthly wisdom as foolishness (1 Cor. 1:20, 25). The most foolish thing of God has greater depth of wisdom than all the scribes and learned men who have ever graced this planet combined. We could ply people with the mathematical beauty of spiraling galaxies and overwhelm their minds with the wonders of the cosmos, and we would have added nothing to the weight of God's wisdom. The wisdom of man is foolishness to God, and the wisdom of God reeks of foolishness to man. You cannot flood a man's soul with paint and color and canvas and hope he could then build a bridge. Neither could one be filled with the wisdom of the world and be expected to understand God. The two pursuits are separated by too great a chasm. "The word of the cross is foolishness to those who are perishing, but to us who are being saved it is the power [and wisdom] of God" (1 Cor. 1:18).

So Jesus, then, is the culmination of all God's work and wisdom. The story of the cross carries with it untapped treasuries of knowledge. The beauty of the redemptive work wrought through Christ causes those who are dead in sin to rise up alive and new, having cast off all that would have seen them damned to hell. Dead men made live, rescued from the pit by the wisdom of God poured into wicked hearts and minds by the gracious work of the Spirit: that is true power!

We sit here begging God to work in our lives. We weep that we don't sense his power and presence. We long to have some evidence that God still moves. If we have come to know salvation through faith in the work of Jesus, then God has moved. He has already done his highest work in our hearts by the death and resurrection of his son. Think of it this way: if God were to heal our bodies, fill our bank accounts, and warm our affections for him but never bring us near to Jesus, then we would find ourselves finally and fully cast to hell. But if God rends heaven to bring us near to his son who lived and died and lived again for us, then though we die as paupers with plagues in our bodies, we find ourselves finally and fully whole, healed and rich in Christ.

The greatest work of God therefore is the one that lasts when the stars have fallen from their places and the sun has vanished from the sky. When we find ourselves a conglomerate of peoples and languages gathered round the throne to exalt the Lamb thereon, we will not praise him for the groceries or the putting off of disease, but we will with unified voices cry out, "Worthy are you for you were slain, and by your blood you ransomed people for God from every tribe and language and people and nation" (Rev. 5:9).

You wonder if God still moves, and the answer is found in the evidence that you who once did not know God have come to know him and be known by him. He has loved you with love everlasting and has taught you to love him in return. He has pierced the hardened heart and opened up eyes formerly blind so you could be made like him. Think about that—God is making you to be like him! He is causing you to be conformed to the likeness of his Son, and he will carry that to fruition on the day Jesus breaks through the sky. There is no greater work than this.

Read Genesis 1:26–27. What was God's intent for mankind?

_____

_____

Of course, even though God sought people to image him, through sin, the beautiful image of God was marred in us. Still, we know we cannot only regain the likeness of God through faith in Jesus, but we will one day be made fully like Christ.

Read Romans 8:29, Ephesians 4:22–24, Philippians 1:6, 1 Corinthians 15:49, and 1 John 3:1–2.

What kind of hope or encouragement do you take from these verses?

_____

_____

_____

_____

Read Ephesians 2:1–10. This is a rich text full of language outlining who we were before we came to know Jesus and who we are after coming to know Jesus. You will note that the text mentions twice that apart from Christ people are dead, but through Christ, we have been made alive with him. Of course, in the Old and New Testaments, we see prophets, apostles, and Jesus himself bringing the physically dead to life. Often, we are led to believe that a physical resurrection is more significant than a spiritual resurrection. Why is spiritual soul regeneration the most important thing that can happen in an individual's life?

_____

_____

_____

_____

Read Romans 6:1–4 and 2 Corinthians 5:14–21. What do you think it means when the texts say things like "raised to walk in newness of life" or "he is a new creation"? I have actually seen God provide financially for me in miraculous, unexplained ways. I have seen people who should not be able to speak talk as though nothing was wrong. I have seen bodies healed of various diseases. Still, the greatest thing is that a man, woman, or child would move from death to life, from enemy of God to friend, from old nature to new nature. My pocket could overflow with money and my body with health, but if I don't know Jesus, I still pass from this life straight into hell. All the so-called great proofs of God's work have come to mean nothing for my eternity if I do not know and boast in the cross.

As a Pharisee, Paul was uniquely educated in the Scripture and could have flooded the people he taught with all sorts of wisdom. Instead, he chose to avoid lofty speech and wisdom. Read 1 Corinthians 2:1–3. What was it Paul chose to know among the Corinthians?

_____

The Galatian churches had ceased to rely upon the work of God in their lives and had traded it for legalistic practices. Paul rebuked them sharply in the book of Galatians and challenged them to boast in Jesus alone. Read Galatians 6:14–16.

When considering these two passages from Corinthians and Galatians, with what do we find Paul was most concerned not only for new believers but for those who had long been Christians?

_____

_____

What are some tangible earthly blessings you have seen God work in your life or in those friends who are near to you?

_____

_____

_____

_____

Why do we find it easier to boast in those things than in the everlasting work of God through the cross?

_____

_____

_____

_____

What are some ways that we might train ourselves to have an attitude more like Paul's?

_____

_____

_____

_____

Do you typically think of your salvation story as an inspiring story or not-so-inspiring one?

_____

What needs to change in your thinking so you can be reminded that the saving work of God is equally beautiful in all situations?

_____

_____

_____

Who led you to the Lord and when?

_____

When was the last time you shared your salvation story with someone?

_____

What kinds of things keep you from sharing your story?

_____

_____

_____

_____

How can we know that the greatest work God will ever do in our lives is our salvation?

_____

_____

_____

_____

Take some time in prayer and thank God for the work he has done in your life. Take special note of the work God has done in bringing you to salvation.

_____

_____

_____

_____

The Work of God
through the Church

The purpose of this book is that you would be reminded that God is still moving. It isn't my hope that you would finish the book and think to yourself what a nice story it is and how pleased you are that things have turned out well for Inguna. If you aren't careful, you will do exactly that. You will put your coffee down on top of the book and lean back in your chair, satisfied that God is moving in Inguna's life. But later in the day, while you are filling out paperwork at the office or picking up the milk—whole for the kids but 1 percent for yourself—you will find yourself wondering why God isn't moving in your life. That nagging question will again sit there in your brain, and the satisfaction you realized earlier in the day will be replaced with hot bitterness that taunts and keeps you awake all night. If you have not yet seen the encouragement in this book, you may need to start over; perspective is everything.

Remember that the greatest, highest, most impressive work God will ever do in you or in me is that he graciously gave us salvation. In the second section of the book, we have found that the next greatest work of God is the love commonly shared among believers. I've been loved by my Christian brethren as I've traveled to India, Spain, Czech Republic, Indonesia, and, yes, now to Latvia. The bond I feel as I meet these brothers and sisters for the first time is inexplicable. A hand laid upon one's shoulder by a stranger is odd, especially for me since I value my space; but take me around the world and walk me into a Christian home, and if they embrace me, it feels right. We are, together, part of the whole. Our love is not dutiful but rather an overflow of the person of Christ who has worked so efficiently and completely in us such that we resemble him in all things. Even as I write this chapter, cruel attacks are being carried out on our Christian family around the world with videos posted online of men being beheaded. Women are being dragged from their homes and raped. Children are fleeing into the mountains to escape their tormentors and are dying of thirst there. I have never met them, but my heart is crushed for them. I ache deep in my belly for them, and our church is regularly praying for them. They are part of us. We speak in different languages and have wildly different cultures, but we worship the same God and were bought by the same blood. The way God worked in my heart for salvation he has worked also in theirs. I love them. Other such tragedies are carried out on a global scale constantly, but none pierce me as deeply as those that strike at the heart of my Christian family.

It is true that the church is often a poor example of love, and should someone like Paul walk into our homes after having been converted, we would likely despise and scorn him for his former conduct. We'd remind him of his sinfulness and shame. We'd probably tell him how he arrested our cousin or put to death our niece, and we'd serve him with a scowl. We have become quite mean. Sure, not everyone in church is mean, but there is a hardness that seems to pervade church culture anymore. We are cynical and skeptical, and we are guilty of keeping great records of wrong. We smile at their faces and disparage against them behind their backs. Such a wicked attitude is largely due to a misunderstanding of salvation. We think ourselves too holy, and we find others too filthy. We forget that the work of salvation in their lives was just as miraculous as it was in ours. We overlook that being made new is the sole work of God in and through us by the blood of his Son and the influence of his Spirit. Too often we have commended ourselves for our righteousness and have applauded our own work, refusing to remember that we added nothing to this change that has taken place. We would naturally be better lovers of the brethren if we recalled often the truth of our adversarial state prior to Christ.

But misunderstanding salvation or thinking too highly of ourselves only contributes to some of the lack of love and affection we see in our churches. Another reason the church fails to love its own well is we have come to believe it is more important to love those outside the church. The general attitude is if someone is a believer and already among us, I must now turn my love and attention to those who do not yet know Jesus. While it sounds noble and true, it is, unfortunately for the state of the church, both unbiblical thinking and counterproductive. Let me explain.

Jesus never tells us it is our love for those outside the church that proves us as his disciples; it is exactly the opposite. Jesus says in John 13:34–35, "A new commandment I give to you, that you love one another: just as I have loved you, you also are to love one another. By this all people will know that you are my disciples, if you have love for one another." It is the last night of the life of Christ. He has gathered his disciples in the upper room. Jesus has already humbled himself and adorned himself in nothing but a towel and moved through the room washing the feet of his disciples. They eat the bread and drink from the cup, and he institutes the Lord's Supper. Then he tells them to love one another. This isn't a speech to the crowds. He isn't traveling through the busy streets of Jericho preaching to all the people, nor is he shouting from a boat to a shore crowded with passersby. Judas has already left to put into motion the betrayal of Christ. Jesus's hour is now at hand, and he tells his disciples the way the world will know they are believers is that they love one another well. Love each other well.

Paul, when writing to the churches of Galatia, reminds them, "You were called to freedom, brothers. Only do not use your freedom as an opportunity for the flesh, but through love serve one another. For the whole law is fulfilled in one word: 'You shall love your neighbor as yourself.' But if you bite and devour one another, watch out that you are not consumed by one another" (Gal. 5:13–15). The churches in this region are dealing with legalism, and though they gained salvation through the work of God by the Spirit, they are now seeking to do things of their own volition. Paul is cautioning and reminding them of the freedom they have in Christ but also reminding them to be loving toward each other so they will not be consumed by one another. Don't we feel that too many times today the church is biting and devouring one another rather than loving one another? This isn't an instruction on how to treat those outside the body of Christ. Paul is fiercely concerned with the way believers treat other believers.

Paul says again in Corinthians,

> If I speak in the tongues of men and of angels, but have not love, I am a noisy gong or a clanging cymbal. And if I have prophetic powers, and understand all mysteries and all knowledge, and if I have all faith,

so as to move mountains, but have not love, I am nothing. If I give away all that I have, and if I deliver up my body to be burned, but have not love, I gain nothing. Love is patient and kind; love does not envy or boast; it is not arrogant or rude. It does not insist on its own way; it is not irritable or resentful; it does not rejoice at wrongdoing, but rejoices with the truth. Love bears all things, believes all things, hopes all things, endures all things. Love never ends. (1 Cor. 13:1–8)

This text is read at almost every wedding, and while it is certainly reasonable to use it in such a fashion, it is important to understand the context. Corinthians is a letter to people who belong to the faith. In chapters 12 through 14, Paul is dealing with the use of spiritual gifts within the church. (We will cover this more in the next section.) When Paul speaks of love here in Corinthians, he has in mind an instruction to believers and their conduct among other believers. This isn't a general instruction on love but rather specifically how one believer should use his or her gifts among other believers.

Take it a step further, and we find in 1 John over and over that a measure of salvation is our love for the brethren. We know John wrote this to believers so they would know they were saved (5:13), but if we were to make a list of the different proofs of salvation mentioned, we will find that leading the list is the love we have for one another:

> Whoever says he is in the light and hates his brother is still in darkness. Whoever loves his brother abides in the light, and in him there is no cause for stumbling. But whoever hates his brother is in the darkness and walks in the darkness, and does not know where he is going, because the darkness has blinded his eyes. (1 John 2:9–11)

The argument could be made that the Greek word translated here as "brother" could mean humanity as a whole. After all, the word can mean flesh-and-blood brother, familial member, believer, half brother, and humankind. If it could mean each of these, then how do we know which is intended here in 1 John? That becomes an understanding of context. John, writing so people can know they've inherited salvation, speaks of loving "one another" and "*the* brothers." He says the "beloved" should "love one another." We know those who are in Christ Jesus are the beloved (Col. 3:12). John speaks further that we should love those who have been born of God: "By this it is evident who are the children of God, and who are the children of the devil: whoever does not practice righteousness is not of God, nor is the one who does not love his brother. For this is the message that you have heard from the beginning, that we should love one another" (1 John 3:10–11). He continues,

> We know that we have passed out of death into life, because we love the brothers. Whoever does not love abides in death. Everyone who hates his brother is a murderer, and you know that no murderer has eternal life abiding in him. By this we know love, that he laid down his life for us, and we ought to lay down our lives for the brothers. But if anyone has the world's goods an d sees his brother in need, yet closes his heart against him, how does God's love abide in him? Little children, let us not love in word or talk but in deed and in truth. (1 John 3:14–18)

John repeats this idea of loving the brethren well over and over again in this short book. "Beloved, let us love one another, for love is from God, and whoever loves has been born of God and knows God. Anyone who does not love does not know God, because God is love" (1 John 4:7–8). "Beloved, if God so loved us, we also ought to love one another. No one has ever seen God; if we love one another, God abides in us and his love is perfected in us" (1 John 4:11–12). "Everyone who believes that Jesus is the Christ has been born of God, and everyone who loves the Father loves whoever has been born of him" (1 John 5:1).

When we love one another well within the church, we find evidence that we are truly walking in the light of God; we prove we are children of God. We are confident by our love for one another that we have passed from death to life. Don't get me wrong. I'm not saying we should be cold or distant to those who are not part of the body of Christ. Quite the contrary. Luke instructs us to do the following:

> I say to you who hear, love your enemies, do good to those who hate you, bless those who curse you, pray for those who abuse you. If you love those who love you, what benefit is that to you? For even sinners love those who love them. And if you do good to those who do good to you, what benefit is that to you? For even sinners do the same. But love your enemies, and do good, and lend, expecting nothing in return, and your reward will be great, and you will be sons of the Most High, for he is kind to the ungrateful and the evil. Be merciful, even as your Father is merciful. (Luke 6:27-36)

Certainly we should be good to those who don't know God in hopes they come to know him, but we should be especially good to those who belong to God's household: "So then, as we have opportunity, let us do good to everyone, and especially to those who are of the household of faith" (Gal. 6:10). Inguna was loved well by the church, and it changed the trajectory of her life. When the church loves and cherishes its own, we find people who thrive as they embrace the truth and power of God. When we have been loved well by the church, we have been strengthened and made stouthearted. But when we've been treated lightly, we have been wounded deeply.

The church of God was created by God to show his glory and beauty. We pound the table and raise our voices to the heavens begging God to move in our lives, pleading him to show himself to us in a mighty way. We feel certain we've been forgotten. But God has worked among us and continues to do so. He has lavished on us the grace of redemption through the cross and has built for himself a bride beautiful and resplendent, of which we are part. We were loved to this place we are now in. We were pulled along with cords of affection by those who have gone before us, and we have been cradled in the embrace of discipleship. We wonder if God still moves, and we need look no further than the one who led us to the Lord or the one who paid for our coffee yesterday while listening to our woes. We look at those who gather round our sick bed, and we hear the reports of the faithful who prayed this past Wednesday on our behalf, and we must know God still works. The text at the timely moment that reads, "Praying for you" or the email that says, "God put you on my heart today" are bountiful ways in which the church is rising up around us to show us the love of God.

Yes, God still works among us. When a Texas Sunday school class loved a Latvian woman well, it resulted in a school on the other side of the world. When those who had been hunted previously by Paul showed him great compassion, it resulted in a prolific preacher and writer to whom we look for wisdom nearly any time we open up the New Testament. When we were loved well, it brought us to Jesus, grew us in him, and strengthened us to press on regardless of tomorrow's uncertainties.

Beloved, God is working in your life today!

Take some time today and read through 1 John. Underline or highlight each mention John makes of loving the brothers, or by contrast hating the brothers. You will want to give yourself at least half an hour to go through the book.

What does John say about those who don't love the brothers?

_____

_____

_____

_____

If we lack love for those who are part of the Christian family, what does that indicate about our love for God?

_____

_____

How many different verses/times does John mention the love of the brethren as an indication that someone is truly saved?

_____

Read Acts 9:26–30. How did Barnabas show love to Paul?

_____

_____

Read Philippians 4:10–20. How did the Philippian church show love to Paul?

_____

_____

What would have to take place in your life for you to believe God is really at work?

_____

_____

_____

_____

Name two or three people who have loved you well and poured something of Jesus into your life.

_____

_____

Name one or two people to whom you are currently showing the love of Jesus (or one or two people to whom you could be showing love).

_____

_____

How is your church excelling at showing each other the love of God?

_____

_____

_____

_____

Why do you think so many churches are failing today at showing one another love?

_____

_____

_____

_____

Are there needs in your small group/Bible study/Sunday school class going unmet?

_____

_____

_____

_____

What are some things you can do personally to show people within your church the love of God more clearly?

_____

_____

_____

_____

The Provision of the Father for His Children

When we consider the provision of God for his people, we must be careful that we don't simply relegate God to a cosmic genie. God provides for his people so he can be more highly glorified and so we can see him more clearly. Consider also that God provides for us in many ways and not just the ones we might deem miraculous. Frequently, God will use those he has called together as his body to meet the physical or spiritual needs of individuals within the church. Again, this isn't for the exaltation of the church but rather to demonstrate the glorious work of God in the hearts of the men and women who belong to him.

On Paul's second missionary journey, he traveled to Corinth and "found a Jew named Aquila, a native of Pontus, recently come from Italy with his wife Priscilla, and because he was of the same trade he stayed with them and worked, for they were tentmakers by trade" (Acts 18:2–3). Paul certainly hadn't always been a tentmaker; he had been a chief Pharisee. He was part of the ruling class in Jerusalem. Perhaps he had learned the skill as a child, or maybe he had gleaned it along the way in his travels, but he viewed it as the means by which God provided for him. Making tents freed him to preach the gospel of Christ without ever being a financial burden to the young but burgeoning churches. But Paul knew he had the right to receive payment and financial support among those whom he sowed the gospel.

> If we have sown spiritual things among you, is it too much if we reap material things from you? If others share this rightful claim on you, do not we even more? Nevertheless, we have not made use of this right, but we endure anything rather than put an obstacle in the way of the gospel of Christ. Nor am I writing these things to secure any such provision. For I would rather die than have anyone deprive me of my ground for boasting. What then is my reward? That in my preaching I may present the gospel free of charge, so as not to make full use of my right in the gospel. (1 Corinthians 9:11–18)

Paul worked hard to preach the gospel free of charge, but this is not because he was against the church supporting those who labored at the work of preaching God's gospel. To the contrary, when he was first at Antioch before he had even left with Barnabas on his first missionary journey, the two of them had been charged with carrying a gift from Antioch to Judea: "So the disciples determined, everyone according to his ability, to send relief to the brothers living in Judea. And they did so, sending it to the elders by the hand of Barnabas and Saul" (Acts 12:29–30). Furthermore, as we shall see in a moment, Paul was instrumental in securing gifts from the Corinthian church for the benefit of the saints in Jerusalem. If these were not enough, in the passage already quoted we find the following:

> Who serves as a soldier at his own expense? Who plants a vineyard without eating any of its fruit? Or who tends a flock without getting some of the mild? Do I say these things on human authority? Does not the Law say the same? For it is written in the Law of Moses, 'You shall not muzzle an ox when it treads out the grain.' Is it for oxen that God is concerned? Does he not speak entirely for our sake? It was written for our sake, because the plowman should plow in hope and the thresher thresh in hope of sharing in the crop. If we have sown spiritual things among you, is it too much if we reap material things from you? (1 Cor. 9:7–11)

So we conclude then that Paul bore no ill will to those who received financial resources having first proclaimed the Bible, and actually, he encouraged the church to supply the needs of the saints. He worked hard at tent making and was confident in the provision of God for all his needs.

Still, there were times when tent making was not sufficient to supply even the basic things Paul required.

> I rejoiced in the Lord greatly that now at length you have revived your concern for me. You were indeed concerned for me, but you had no opportunity. Not that I am speaking of being in need, for I have learned in whatever situation I am to be content. I know how to be brought low, and I know how to abound. In any and every circumstance, I have learned the secret of facing plenty and hunger, abundance and need. I can do all things through him who strengthens me. Yet it was kind of you to share my trouble. And you Philippians yourselves know that in the beginning of the gospel, when I left Macedonia, no church entered into partnership with me in giving and receiving, except you only. Even in Thessalonica you sent me help for my needs once and again. Not that I seek the gift, but I seek the fruit that increases to your credit. I have received full payment, and more I am well supplied, having received from Epaphroditus the gifts you sent, a fragrant offering, a sacrifice acceptable and pleasing to God. And my God will supply every need of yours according to his riches in glory in Christ Jesus. To our God and Father be glory forever and ever. Amen. (Phil. 4:10–20)

From Paul, we learn several wonderful things. Need is tempered by contentment. When one is completely content in Christ, need is no longer measured in terms of plenty or hunger, abundance or lack. Contentment is therefore greater than need. Paul recognizes he can face all circumstances through God who strengthens him. (Philippians 4:13 has nothing to do with football games, rock climbing, or test taking; rather, it has everything to do with contentment, whether our plates are overflowing or we have but a stale crust of bread to sustain us.) Paul recognizes the kindness of the Philippians who generously cared for him not only when he was with them but even when he was preaching in Thessalonica. Paul then encourages them with the reminder that God will fully supply every need they might ever have. No man would say such a thing in good conscience and with sincere confidence if he had not first experienced such rich truth himself.

The provision we see God making for Paul can offer tremendous encouragement to us as well. God takes care of those who belong to him. He always has. In Matthew, Jesus reminds his disciples, "Do not be anxious about your life, what you will eat or what you will drink, nor about your body, what you will put on. Is not life more than food, and the body more than clothing?" (6:25). In the following lines of the text, he has his disciples consider how well cared for are the birds of the air: "They neither sow nor reap nor gather into barns, and yet your heavenly Father feeds them. Are you not of more value than they?"(6:26). Jesus asks the disciples to consider the apparel of the lilies of the field, which are more beautifully adorned than Solomon ever was in his glory, and inquires, "If God so clothes the grass of the field, which today is alive and tomorrow is thrown into the oven, will he not much more clothe you, O you of little faith?" (6:30). Jesus reminds them that even pagans are looking for food and clothing. This is an obvious thing to God. He has not overlooked the fact that his people need to be cared for and assures, "Your heavenly Father knows that you need them all. But seek first the kingdom of God and his righteousness, and all these things will be added to you" (6:33). We make up all kinds of answers as to what "all these things" might mean, but the text tells us it means food and clothing. This isn't a passage about new cars and expensive watches. God will give us all the food and clothing we need to be sustained. God will meet our needs, though it may not always take the form we desire.

Read Matthew 6:19–34. We tend not to read verses 19–24 when preaching the birds and flowers text, but the two texts are tied together. You will notice the first six verses deal with not pursuing temporary treasure or money. Of course, Jesus seems to anticipate the argument "But we need food and clothing, don't we?" So Jesus responds by highlighting for them how faithful God is to the birds and to the flowers. Certainly, if God can supply the needs of sparrows and lilies, then he can supply the needs of his saints.

In Exodus 12, we see God liberate his people from 430 years of slavery in Egypt, and he does so with an incredible display of his power. For the next forty years, he feeds his people with manna in the wilderness. Manna is the spiritual bread that would appear every morning around the camp of the Israelites. It was extremely perishable and would melt in the heat of the day or rot and stink if kept overnight. There was one exception; every week on the day before the Sabbath, there would be enough manna for the people to be sustained for two days since God would provide nothing on the Sabbath day. This particular manna would last overnight with no threat of worms or maggots. God would sustain his people.

It should also be noted that this wasn't a small tribe walking through the desert. There were more than six hundred thousand men, which doesn't even count the women or children. Just three weeks into their forty-year journey, they became thirsty and groaned and bellyached against the God of heaven who had so dynamically just saved them. His solution was for Moses to strike a rock with a staff and have enough water flow forth to quench the thirst of the people and beasts in the camp. God would sustain his people.

When the desert exile came to a close, Moses reminded the people that God "humbled you and let you hunger and fed you with manna, which you did not know, nor did your fathers know, that he might make you know that man does not live by bread alone, but man lives by every word that comes from the mouth of the Lord. Your clothing did not wear out on you and your foot did not swell these forty years" (Deut. 8:3–4). God not only provided the food necessary to sustain them, but he ensured their clothes would not wear out. What were "all these things" Jesus promised to those who sought God in Matthew 6? Was it not food and clothing? We find when the people finally did enter into the promised land and were able to be sustained by the food that grew in abundance there, "the manna ceased the day after they ate of the produce of the land. And there was no longer manna for the people of Israel, but they ate of the fruit of the land of Canaan that year" (Josh. 5:12). God would sustain his people.

When God's prophet Elijah fled into the wilderness to hide from his pursuers, God said, "Hide yourself by the brook Cherith, which is east of the Jordan. You shall drink from the brook, and I have commanded the ravens to feed you there" (1 Kings 17:3–4). And when the brook inevitably dried up from the drought God brought to the land, he instructed, "Go to Zarephath, which belongs to Sidon, and dwell there. Behold, I have commanded a widow there to feed you" (1 Kings 17:8–9). God would sustain his prophet.

Paul, when condemning false teachers, points out that one of their motivations for teaching is rooted in financial gain, but Paul paints the godly picture when he says, "There is great gain in godliness with contentment, for we brought nothing into the world, and we cannot take anything out of the world. But if we have food and clothing, with these we will be content" (1 Tim. 6:6–8). God would sustain his preacher.

There has never been a question as to whether God would supply the need for his people sufficient to sustain them in all things pertaining to God's holy work and purpose. He has always faithfully done so. There are faults within our own hearts and wicked appetites that will, on occasion, keep us from being supplied with food and clothing. These are not at all the fault of God, nor should we seek to blame others.

Sometimes the reason we are in dire straits is because we have violated the word of God. Perhaps we have dishonored God through our work or our finances. Sometimes we are simply too lazy. The Bible uses the term "sluggard" to describe those who are idle. If sluggardly ways and slovenly habits abound in us, then we should not think God would sustain us in such circumstances. We need only read Proverbs to see how God feels about the sluggard.

Read Proverbs 6:9–11, 13:4, 15:19, 20:4, 21:25 and 24:30–34.

What are some of the attitudes that seem to pervade the life of a sluggard?

_____

_____

_____

_____

What sort of instruction might we receive from the sluggard so we can live a more upright life?

_____

_____

_____

_____

Did you notice that the sluggard still expects to find a harvest even though he has done no plowing or sowing? It is clear from the text that the sluggard craves but gains nothing, and thorns block all his paths. He is always looking for an opportunity to rest his hands, and the end result is that poverty comes upon him.

Those among us who are careless and lazy and think that God will rescue us in one fell swoop would do well to remember the tent making of Paul mentioned above. God sustains us and makes us able to be sustained. If he gives us the field and the seed, and we leave the field unkempt and the seed to rot, we can hardly hold God responsible for our lack of sustenance.

But I am not, in this writing, concerned so much with those who find being sustained difficult due to sinful laziness. Rather, what about those who serve God with vigor and faithfulness and still find their bellies cramping in hunger? What of those who shiver in the night for lack of substantial clothing? Paul was certainly such a man, wasn't he? We need only read the Philippians 4 or 2 Corinthians 11 to find that Paul readily admits to being in want, being naked, and hungry. If God truly gives "all these things" to those who seek first his kingdom, what should we make of such a truth? Deuteronomy is helpful in explaining, "He humbled you and let you hunger and fed you with manna, which you did not know, nor did your fathers know, that he might make you know that man does not live by bread alone, but man lives by every word that comes from the mouth of the Lord" (8:3). Just two verses later, the people of God are reminded, "Know then in your heart that, as a man disciplines his son, the Lord your God disciplines you" (8:5). We ought not to think of discipline here in terms of a consequence for sinful behavior but rather in terms of learning self-control and the discipline to carry oneself in a certain way. When Hebrews 12 speaks of discipline, it reminds us that the end of godly discipline is sharing in "his holiness" (12:10) and that it "later yields the peaceful fruit of righteousness" (12:11) by those who have received its instruction. Moses, in Deuteronomy, lets the people know they had to eat manna for forty years to learn to trust in the word and promise of God more than they did their daily food.

Paul faced such violent affliction in Asia so he could be a comfort to those who faced similar violent affliction and so he would rely not on himself but "on God who raises the dead" (2 Cor. 1:3–9). Furthermore, though he pleaded with God to remove the thorn in his flesh, God saw fit to allow this "messenger of Satan" to remain so God's great grace and power could be demonstrated in Paul's life (2 Cor. 12:6–10).

We see, then, that God fully sustains his people, save for those moments when limiting or even removing the supply causes the individual to know God better, trust him more fully, be more conformed to his likeness, or offer comfort to those who have faced similar devastation. Even Jesus, when having eaten nothing for forty days and facing temptation from the Devil, refused to make bread for his aching belly since he already knew the lesson of loving God's word more deeply than food (Matt. 4:4). Food is good for the body—but not better for the body than obeying God's commands. Read Matthew 4:1–10.

So we find we are not provided for as we think either because we are sinful or because God is growing us, but there is a third option: sometimes we aren't cared for because the church of God is in sin.

As we have already indicated, it was apparent that Paul was not only sustained by his tent making but also through the generous care of the church. In 2 Corinthians, we find an interesting teaching from Paul concerning the gifts and offerings of the church. Chapters 8–9 deal with a gift that the Corinthian church had previously promised to provide for the aid of the saints in Jerusalem. However, as the time drew near to give the financial gift, the Corinthian church realized it was far less than anticipated and—so as not to embarrass itself—decided to withhold the gift altogether.

Paul rebukes the church at Corinth and indicates the poorer Macedonian church had overflowed with generosity when it had heard of the generous nature of the Corinthians.

Paul says, "In a severe test of affliction, their abundance of joy and their extreme poverty have overflowed in a wealth of generosity on their part. For they gave according to their means, as I can testify, and beyond their means, of their own free will, begging us earnestly for the favor of taking part in the relief of the saints" (2 Cor. 8:2–4). Paul lets the Corinthians know that soon he will be coming to receive their gift and that some Macedonians will be coming with him. The situation here isn't that the Corinthians didn't want to help the saints in Jerusalem, but they were embarrassed by the size of their gift. Paul encourages them when he says, "If the readiness is there, it is acceptable according to what a person has, not according to what he does not have" (2 Cor. 8:12). Paul goes on to say he isn't asking the Corinthians to give until they are in need themselves but rather to meet a need out of their current abundance. He explains, "I do not mean that others should be eased and you burdened, but that as a matter of fairness your abundance at the present time should supply their need, so that their abundance may supply your need, that there may be fairness. As it is written, 'Whoever gathered much had nothing left over, and whoever gathered little had no lack'" (2 Cor. 8:13–14).

One of the things we should recognize right away is that Paul's instruction isn't given so much that it hurts or impoverishes you. We have people who write and teach that way today, saying that if you aren't giving in a way that costs you something, then you are disobeying God. Paul's gist is, "Give out of the abundance you have. I'm not interested in you becoming burdened through your giving." Some of us only have five dollars of surplus while others have thousands. Give the surplus. There will shortly come a time when we have a lack, and at that time, those with surplus can serve us. That is the fairness of which Paul speaks.

An argument that we are to give something that costs us is often raised when considering 1 Chronicles 21:24, where King David says he would not offer to the Lord something that cost him nothing. Ornan had offered to the king the use of his oxen and threshing floor at no costs so that David could make an offering to God who has just withdrawn his hand of judgment. However, David refuses to offer something of Ornan's to God. David knows he himself is guilty of the sin that brought the hand of God against the people, so the sacrifice must be of his own offering. Therefore, David buys the land and the oxen from Ornan. The price paid was a pittance for a king. David did not suffer financially when he made the offering to God, but it was an offering of that which was now his own.

God's gracious design is that the church would provide for the church. When one is lacking in food or clothing, it is most certainly the case that another has a surplus that should be made available. The quote Paul references in 8:14 is from Exodus, and it deals specifically with God's provision of manna. We find that when the people would go out to gather the manna, "They gathered, some more, some less. But when they measured it with an omer, whoever gathered much had nothing left over, and whoever gathered little had no lack" (Ex. 16:17–18). The idea is that God supplied the resources to meet the needs of his people. Some gathered much and some gathered little, but when all was measured out and divided, there was no lack. It isn't any different today. God supplies his people with enough resources to clothe and feed all those who belong to him, and often those resources come through other believers. Some have much and others little, but there is no reason for there to be lack among us if we are working faithfully as the body of Christ. Don't we see this truth unfold for Inguna? Those who had plenty met her need. The Macedonians met Paul's need. We've had people meet our needs. We even recognize there have been times when our paltry surplus has been sufficient to meet the need of someone else. Sometimes we have just enough of a surplus to buy a toothbrush.

We never again need wonder if God is moving among us, for he has richly provided the cross, the love of the brethren, and our daily food. We believe God is absent because we think too little of the bread on our tables, the shirts on our backs, and, yes, even our very salvation. We cash our paychecks and measure the work we've done and wonder wickedly in our hearts when God will do something. Oh, beloved and chosen child of God, he has done something already! God still sustains his people.

What specifically is meant by "all these things" in Matthew 6?

_____

_____

_____

_____

What are some other texts that also speak of food and clothing in a similar manner?

_____

_____

How is God providing your daily need right now?

_____

_____

_____

_____

Can you think of a time you've seen your church provide for the needs of yourself or another member?

_____

_____

Has there been a time when sluggardly behavior has put you or your family in a bind?

_____

_____

Is there something you can do now to be a better steward of your money?

_____

_____

Is there surplus in your budget you can use to meet another's need?

_____

Have you ever seen God supply a need in what you might consider a supernatural way?

_____

_____

_____

_____